# Look Who's Learning to Read

**50** Fun Ways to Instill a Love of Reading in Young Children

## SHELLEY HARWAYNE

**SCHOLASTIC**

New York • Toronto • London • Auckland • Sydney
Mexico City • New Delhi • Hong Kong • Buenos Aires

*With great love for Andie, Ben, Will, and Zach,*

*our wonderful grandchildren,*

*who adorn the cover,*

*and for Sasha Ruby,*

*who arrived after the photograph was taken*

Cover design: Maria Lilja
Interior design: LDL Designs
Acquiring Editor: Lois Bridges
Production Editor: Carol Ghiglieri
Copy Editor: Shea Dean

ISBN-13: 978-0-545-05894-0
ISBN-10: 0-545-05894-5

# Table of Contents

## LANGUAGE PLAY

## BEGINNING WRITING

## APPENDIX

# Dear Readers,

The book you hold in your hand is intended to support you as you help young children feel at home in the world of literacy from the very first day they turn the pages of a book until the day they blow out five candles and are able to read the messages on their birthday cakes.

In other words, this book is filled with ways to prepare toddlers, preschoolers, and kindergartners to take to literacy as easily as ducks to water. The activities are varied, some working best with one child at a time, others engaging two or three children at once. Many can be easily adapted to small-group and whole-class instruction in preschool and kindergarten classrooms. The activities also accomplish a wide range of goals. Some help youngsters learn the alphabet, while others help children connect sounds with letters or appreciate that words have syllables. Many help youngsters learn to listen for and produce rhymes and develop a love of literature. Still other activities help children recognize words on sight, build vocabulary and concepts, and begin to write on their own. Some of the activities are appropriate for 2-year-olds; others will work better for 3-, 4-, 5-, or even 6-year-olds.

Throughout the book, I have attempted to honor a few simple principles.

- ◆ Children need choice. They love to be part of making decisions.

- ◆ Children deserve the finest of literature. We need to be fussy about the books we borrow or buy for them.

- ◆ Children need to laugh, every day. And their silly sense of humor often differs from ours.

- ◆ Children learn language quite remarkably, so there is no need to use baby talk or water down our choice of words.

- ◆ Children learn that ways of talking in school often differ from ways of talking in the playground or at home. We can help them experience a wide range of ways to use language.

- ◆ Children need to be commended for working hard. Those who make strong efforts accept great challenges.

- ◆ Children need to know that we think they are clever when they ask questions, not simply when they answer questions.

- ◆ Children love rituals—ways of living that are repeated over and over again.

- ◆ Children can learn empathy—feeling for others—at a very early age.

In addition, in selecting which activities to include in this collection, I followed these three guidelines:

1. All activities are grounded in what I know to be true about how children learn to read and write.
2. All activities are joyful, inexpensive, and true to the spirit of childhood.
3. All activities have been field-tested by Grandma Shelley and my beloved grandbabies Andie, Ben, Will, and Zach. (Sasha, grandchild number five, was born as I was completing this book, but together with her sister, brother, parents, grandparents, great-grandparents, aunts, uncles, cousins, babysitters, and teachers, I shall extend to her a gracious and loving welcome into the world of literacy).

I knew that I would take great delight in becoming a grandparent, but I never anticipated becoming so involved, so committed, and so thoroughly in love with my children's children. Following in my husband's footsteps, I retired to become an almost full-time caregiver to our grandchildren. Some might say, and some actually did, that I was overqualified for my position. I had been a mother, of course, but then went on to become an elementary school teacher, an elementary school principal, and finally, a school superintendent in New York City. Taking care of five preschoolers (not all at the same time) seemed a much easier task than watching over the 106,000 students in kindergarten through high school who had been left in my care. In fact, my babysitting days *are* easier than those spent leading a school district, but they are never easy. Providing quality day care is exhilarating and exhausting at the same time. I am often tired at the end of the day. Still, caring for my grandchildren remains the best job I have ever had.

Throughout my career, I have taken a very strong professional interest in the teaching of reading and writing, publishing many texts for teachers along the way. It will come as no surprise, then, to hear that much of what I do with these very young children supports their becoming successful readers and writers when the time is right for them.

Although this book is filled with literacy-related activities, you can be sure that I spend time with my grandchildren visiting parks, museums, zoos, and playgrounds. We listen to music, dance, create marching bands, prepare snacks, take long walks, roughhouse, and cuddle on the living room sofa. We finger paint, sculpt with clay, watch children's television shows, play dress-up, build with blocks, do puzzles, fiddle around with computer games, and play with the toys that are scattered about the house. All of these childhood activities contribute to children's success as readers and writers; however, the activities that follow deliberately aim at helping youngsters become confident and competent explorers in the world of books—the books they will read and the books they will write.

Whether you are a teacher, a parent, a babysitter, a nanny, a day-care provider, an au pair, or a grandparent, I hope these activities help you spend joyous moments with the children in your care and help those children learn to read and write as naturally as they have been learning to walk and talk.

With great respect for the valuable work you do,

*Shelley Harwayne*

## A Special Note About the Audience

When I first set out to record how I pass the time with my grandchildren, I did so with a parent, grandparent, and babysitter audience in mind. Yet when I shared my ideas with friends who are early childhood teachers, they often responded, "I think I'll try that with my students!" I realized then that my audience needed to include teachers along with caregivers. Clearly, the literacy activities connected to mealtime, bath-time, and bedtime described here are meant to be practiced at home; however, it is my hope that teachers suggest these family activities at parent meetings, use the original rhymes as reading material in their classrooms, and enjoy these home activities with their own young children, grandchildren, nieces, and nephews.

Look Who's Learning to Read

# READING ALOUD

## 1. The Read-Aloud, Of Course

*ACCOMPLISHMENTS: appreciating stories, learning vocabulary and concepts, appreciating illustrations, becoming familiar with the conventions of print*

Of all the activities in this collection, this is the most essential one. Reading aloud to young children is the foundation of all literacy development. Young children who are read aloud to frequently and with pleasure learn how books, stories, and print work. They learn concepts, vocabulary, and information. They learn that reading must make sense and that people always read to make meaning. They learn to ask questions of their reading. They learn that reading can change the way you think about the world and yourself. They learn the meaning of reading between the lines. They learn about the power of illustrations. And most of all, they learn the pleasures of getting lost in a book. This activity is appropriate for all ages.

### MATERIALS TO GATHER

Here, the book being used is *Good Thing You're Not an Octopus!* (Markes); it should be readily available in the children's section of most public libraries. Notes in the Tips to Consider section apply whenever you read aloud to young children. Notes in Invitations to Play refer specifically to this book, but the procedures can be easily adapted to others.

### INVITATIONS TO PLAY

Although reading aloud to children is not considered play in a traditional sense, read-alouds with young children should always be playful and joyful experiences. The invitation described below is offered as an example, as there are no set rules to follow.

◆ Introduce the book.

I have a brand-new book to share with you today. The title is *Good Thing You're Not an*

*Octopus!* Isn't that a funny title? A woman named Julie Markes is the author. She wrote the words. It says right here, "Story by Julie Markes." A woman named Maggie Smith is the illustrator. It says right here, "Pictures by Maggie Smith."

I think it's a good thing *you* are not an octopus. Do you know why? How would your life be different if you were an octopus?

♦ Encourage children to respond. Perhaps they will talk about living in water or eating different foods.

Look at the cover—the picture shows another way your life would be different. Yes, if you wanted to wear clothing, you would have to have very special pants to cover all your tentacles. Yes, those look like legs, but they are called tentacles. You have two legs, but an octopus has eight tentacles.

Let's see what the rest of this book is about.

♦ Read the first page in the most inviting and energetic way you can (see tips below).

♦ Read the rest of the book, stopping after all the pages that announce, "It's a good thing you're not a ___."

Why do you think the author says it's a good thing you're not a caterpillar if you don't like to put your shoes on?

♦ Turn the page to share the answer.

Why do you think she says it's a good thing you're not a baby kangaroo if you don't like to ride in your car seat?

♦ Continue reading the book, encouraging children to linger on the illustrations, offer comments, ask questions, make guesses, and so on.

♦ Offer additional information when appropriate.

It's true caterpillars do have sixteen feet.

Did you know that kangaroos have pouches to carry their babies?

Can you ever imagine eating a worm like a bird does?

♦ Complete the book, making sure that the ending sounds like an ending (see tips below).

## TIPS TO CONSIDER

♦ Be sure to select high-quality books, allowing children to make choices from among the books you present. A list of Favorite Read-Alouds appears in the Appendix along with lists of Must-Know Poets and Must-Know Nonfiction Writers. For more ideas, consult with librarians and bookstore workers as well as online resources devoted to children's literature, including Scholastic's Teach With Caldecott Medal Winners (www2.scholastic.com/browse/article.jsp?id=4512); the Spaghetti Book Club, which features children's reviews of books (spaghettibookclub.org); Reading Rainbow, PBS's index of titles of books turned into televised programs (pbskids.org/readingrainbow); the Association for Library Service to Children's Notable Children's Booklists (alsc.ala.org); and Read That Again, a Web site containing alphabetized lists of wonderful read-alouds (readthatagain.com).

◆ Read all books to yourself before sharing them with children. Be sure the content is appropriate. Make sure you know when to expect the last page in order to read it like an ending (see tip on endings, below).

◆ Eliminate interruptions and distractions as best you can.

◆ Value the read-aloud as a time to sit close and even cuddle.

◆ Be sure to highlight the title of the book, using it to spark conversation.

     The title is the name that the author chose for her book. I wonder why the author chose this title. The book must be about _____.

◆ Point out the name of the author and illustrator, explaining their roles.

     The person who thought up the ideas for this book and wrote the words is called the author. The author of this book is named _____. The artist who makes pictures for books is called the illustrator. The illustrator of this book is named _____.

◆ Share dedications with older children and be sure to explain their purpose.

     Authors work very hard on their books, and when they are finished they often choose to honor someone they love by dedicating the book to that person. This book is dedicated to _____. If you wrote a book, who might you choose to dedicate it to?

◆ Share the first page in a most gracious way, as if you were extending an important invitation, revealing a significant secret, or making an amazing announcement.

◆ Linger on and talk about the illustrations.

◆ Let children know that you read from left to right and from the top of the page to the bottom.

◆ Respond to the books and to the children's comments naturally and enthusiastically.

◆ Encourage children to ask questions, make observations, and offer guesses. In other words, do not allow children to remain passive during a read-aloud.

◆ Ask children questions, not in a testing way but as a means of encouraging conversation.

     Why do you think . . . ? What would you have done . . . ? What do you think would happen if . . . ?

◆ Clarify the meaning of new words and concepts, but do so quickly and simply so as not to interfere with the flow of the story.

◆ Make endings sound like endings, choosing just the kind of drama, pacing, emotion, or pizzazz that feels appropriate to you. Imagine the last page as the curtain coming down on a play.

◆ Reread books frequently and with delight, maintaining the same rhythm and lilt in your voice each time.

◆ Don't limit read-alouds to bedtime; children will benefit from them throughout the day.

◆ Consider creating rituals to accompany the read-aloud (sitting in a favorite chair, turning on a special lamp, reading a set number of books).

◆ Aim to make read-aloud a joyful, precious, and stress-free time together.

◆ Stop reading a book if children seem restless or uninterested.

## POSSIBILITIES TO EXTEND THE LEARNING

- Reread the book as often as children desire. Children gain a lot with each rereading.

- Find nonfiction books to extend understandings about each animal in *Good Thing You're Not an Octopus!*

  > Let's find out if birds eat more than worms.
  >
  > When bears sleep all winter long, it's called hibernation. Let's find out more about those long sleeping times.
  >
  > Let's find out how many teeth shark actually have.

  (When sharing informational texts, be sure to demonstrate how you use the table of contents, index, captions, glossary, chapter headings, and sidebars to gather information.)

- Feel free to innovate on pages in the book. For example, after reading *Good Thing You're Not an Octopus!* you might continue the theme with your own examples:

  > You don't like to drink coffee?
  >
  > It's a good thing you're not Grandma.
  >
  > If you were Grandma, you'd have to drink a big mug of coffee each morning.
  >
  > You don't like to play with trucks?
  >
  > It's a good thing you're not Will.
  >
  > If you were Will, you'd have to play with trucks all afternoon.

- Turn the text into a puppet show, using animal finger puppets.

- Encourage children to retell books to other family members at the end of the day.

- Do other read-aloud activities, including Follow Their Lead, Illustration Peek-a-Boo, Finding Five, Rhyming Read-Alouds, and Hide-and-Seek With Books (see pages 13–22).

- See Appendix for a list of Favorite Read-Alouds grouped by children's ages.

# 2. Follow Their Lead

*ACCOMPLISHMENTS: developing a literary heritage, listening to read-alouds, reading related literature*

In this read-aloud activity, carefully selected books lead to a search for classics in children's literature. The book described below invites children to play "I Spy" with familiar nursery characters and inspires further reading of the poems and stories mentioned. The book also provides opportunities for children to appreciate rhymes. Extension activities introduce children to literary reworkings and parodies. This activity is appropriate for children aged 3 and up.

## MATERIALS TO GATHER

Here, the book being shared is *Each Peach Pear Plum* by Janet and Allan Ahlberg. This popular children's book is readily available in the children's section of most public libraries. Alternative titles are listed in Possibilities to Extend the Learning. Read the Ahlberg book, then ask your librarian to help you gather copies of the other poems and texts mentioned in the book. Track down as many of the references as possible. These include Tom Thumb, Mother Hubbard, Cinderella, the Three Bears, Baby Bunting, Little Bo Peep, Jack and Jill, Robin Hood, and the Wicked Witch from *The Wizard of Oz*.

## INVITATIONS TO PLAY

◆ Introduce the lead book, *Each Peach Pear Plum*.

Today, I have a very special book to share. It's a book that invites you to play "I Spy." You're going to have to look very carefully at the illustrations on each page.

The book was written by Janet and Allan Ahlberg and they drew the illustrations as well.

Are you ready to be good listeners and good observers?

◆ Read the book aloud, asking the children to spot the characters mentioned.

Can you spot a little boy whose name is Tom Thumb?

Can you spot a woman whose name is Mother Hubbard?

Can you spot Cinderella?

◆ Continue reading the rhyming text, helping children find the characters if they are unable to spot them. Some of the characters mentioned will be familiar to the children; other may not be. Feel free to explain the characters as you go along. You can postpone some explanations until the book is complete.

Do you remember the poem about Old Mother Hubbard who went to the cupboard?

Do you remember the movie we saw about Cinderella?

Can you recite "Jack and Jill" with me?

Didn't we once borrow a book from the library about the Three Bears?

I don't think we know much about Tom Thumb, but I have a book that is going to help us get to know him. We will read it later on today.

Robin Hood is a very grown-up story. I think I will tell you about that character later on today instead of reading the book to you.

Do you remember we saw the Wicked Witch when we watched *The Wizard of Oz*?

◆ Reread the book, this time pausing before the rhyming word. Invite children to fill in the missing rhyme. It helps to accentuate the underlined words in the examples which follow.

. . . in the <u>cupboard</u>,
I spy Mother _____ (Hubbard).

. . . down the <u>cellar</u>,
I spy _____ (Cinderella).

. . . on the <u>stairs</u>,
I spy the _____ (Three Bears).

## TIPS TO CONSIDER

◆ Follow the read-aloud tips on pages 10–12.

◆ Do not attempt to read too many follow-up books at any one sitting. It may be enough to simply show the children the books gathered and save the read-alouds for a later time.

◆ Encourage children to recall what they know about the literary characters whenever they are mentioned.

## POSSIBILITIES TO EXTEND THE LEARNING

• Share other picture books that hint at classic stories and rhymes. These include the following:
*1-2-3: A Child's First Counting Book* by Alison Jay
*And the Dish Ran Away with the Spoon* by Janet Stevens and Susan Stevens Crummel
*The Fairy Tale Cake* by Mark Sperring
*Hey, Mama Goose* by Jane Breskin Zalben
*The Jolly Postman or Other People's Letters* by Allan Ahlberg and Janet Ahlberg
*Wait for Me! Said Maggie McGee* by Jean Van Leeuwen

• There are also many takeoffs on fairy tales that serve as joyful companions to the traditional stories. When children hear a familiar story told in a different manner, the essentials of the story structure become crystal clear. They also delight in predicting upcoming events, as they have a general sense of what is going to happen. Ask your librarian for fairy tale takeoffs by Mary Pope Osborne, Diane Stanley, Lisa Campbell Ernst, and Margie Palatini.

# 3. Illustration Peek-a-Boo

*ACCOMPLISHMENTS: paying attention to illustrations, listening to read-alouds*

This read-aloud activity encourages children to pay careful attention to illustrations as they take delight in discovering, inside the text, the illustration that adorns the cover of the book. As you turn to the right page, be prepared for children to gleefully announce, "That's the picture on the cover!" This activity is appropriate for all ages, although not applicable to all books.

## MATERIALS TO GATHER

This activity requires books whose cover illustrations also appear inside. The only way to locate such titles is to note them as you are browsing in the library. Once you demonstrate to children that such a possibility exists, they will be on the lookout for duplicate illustrations.

## INVITATIONS TO PLAY

◆ Select one book with duplicate illustrations. Here, Jane Yolen's *How Do Dinosaurs Eat Their Food?*, is shared. If you choose a different book, let the conversations below serve as a guide.

This book is called *How Do Dinosaurs Eat Their Food?* That's a good question, isn't it? Do you know how they ate their food?

The book was written by a woman named Jane Yolen. I think we have shared many of her books. The illustrations were done by a man named Mark Teague. Look at this beautiful cover. Can you guess what is happening here? Yes, it certainly looks like a dinosaur is going to eat pancakes.

◆ Encourage conversation about the cover, answering children's questions and responding to their comments.

You know, I think that the author and the illustrator were really proud of this illustration. They loved this picture so much that they decided to show it two times, once on the cover and then again on one of the pages inside the book. I am going to read the book to you as we always do, and if you see this picture again, be sure to let me know.

◆ Read the book to children, giving them ample time to delight in the amusing questions and the engaging illustrations.

If children spot the cover illustration inside the book, congratulate them for being good observers. If they don't notice the duplicate illustration, reread the book, giving them another opportunity to spot it.

◆ With 4- and 5-year-olds, you might ask,

Why do you think this illustration was chosen for the cover? Are there other illustrations in the book that would have made a great cover? Why do you think so?

If children are still engaged in read-aloud time, share other selected books.

If children need a change in activity, save the books for another time.

The following popular picture books have cover illustrations that appear inside the books:

Dinosaur Train by John Steven Gurney

Piggies by Don Wood and Audrey Wood

Tumble Bumble by Felicia Bond

◆ Encourage children to flip through pages after reading in order to find the duplicate illustrations on their own.

We can pretend you are on a treasure hunt. Can you flip through these pages, searching for the same picture that is on the cover?

## TIPS TO CONSIDER

◆ Follow read-aloud tips on pages 10–12.

## POSSIBILITIES TO EXTEND THE LEARNING

• Borrow other dinosaur books by Jane Yolen and Mark Teague, including:

How Do Dinosaurs Clean Their Rooms?

How Do Dinosaurs Count to Ten?

How Do Dinosaurs Get Well Soon?

How Do Dinosaurs Go to School?

How Do Dinosaurs Play With Their Friends?

How Do Dinosaurs Say Goodnight?

Have children find out if the cover illustrations on these books appear inside the books as well.

• Share Alison Jay's irresistible board books ABC: A Child's First Alphabet Book and 1-2-3: A Child's First Counting Book. The author/illustrator has tiny hints of upcoming illustrations on every page.

# 4. Finding Five

*ACCOMPLISHMENTS: appreciating nonfiction literature, noting similarities and differences, studying an area of interest*

In this activity, children are offered an array of books based on their interest in a topic, not according to their age or reading abilities. Children are given an opportunity to study, browse, question, and otherwise enjoy books that provide abundant information about the topics they are interested in. They will be asked to find five photographs or illustrations of the same item in five different books. This activity is appropriate for all children with an interest in a topic.

## MATERIALS TO GATHER

The materials for this activity depend on the interests of the children in your care. Here, five books about trucks were shared: Seymour Simon's *Book of Trucks*, Richard Scarry's *Cars and Trucks and Things That Go*, Dorling Kindersley's *My First Truck Board Book*, Byron Barton's *Trucks*, and Philomen Sturges's *I Love Trucks*. Make sure all the books you choose have engaging photographs or illustrations. Sticky notes or bookmarks will also be needed to mark findings.

## INVITATIONS TO PLAY

◆ Introduce your stack of topic-related books.

> Well, I have a special stack of books to share with you today. Since I know that you are so interested in trucks, I have borrowed five picture books about trucks from the library.

◆ Invite children to browse books before reading them aloud.

> Which one would you like to look at first? Do you want me to read the words now or do you want to look through the pages on your own first?

◆ Read books aloud to children when they are finished browsing. If some books have too much text or text that is too sophisticated for the age of the children, share photograph captions and/or retell the contents of longer passages.

◆ Encourage children to offer comments and pose questions.

◆ Attempt to answer their questions.

◆ Begin a treasure hunt activity.

> Since all these books are about trucks, I am going to challenge you to find five dump trucks, one in each book. You can use sticky notes to mark the pages.

◆ When five dump trucks are found, invite children to note details.

> Let's open the books to the pages you have marked and study all these dump trucks. What's the same about them? Do you spot any differences?

◆ Encourage children to pay attention to such qualities as size, color, shape, contents, and printed words on trucks.

◆ Continue this activity by searching for and marking cement mixers, sanitation trucks, fire engines, and so on.

## TIPS TO CONSIDER

◆ Many children's books include suggested audience age levels on their book jackets. Teachers frequently attach a level to the books in their classrooms as well. If children are particularly interested in a topic, however, it is not necessary to keep more advanced books out of their hands. They will learn a great deal from photographs, labels, captions, and conversations with an adult caregiver or teacher.

◆ Ask a librarian for help with creating stacks of books related to your children's current areas of interest. It should be rather easy to find five books on ballet, frogs, baseball, dinosaurs, and the solar system, among other topics.

◆ All books may not have the same contents. Preview the books before suggesting a search. Let children know if some books do not have the desired object.

Only three of these books about ballet show the ballerina doing a grand jeté. Can you find those three pictures?

## POSSIBILITIES TO EXTEND THE LEARNING

• Invite children to carry books with them as you take a neighborhood stroll. Help them identify different kinds of trucks. See Neighborhood Tours on page 90.

• Read other picture books about trucks, including *Good Morning, Digger* by Anne Rockwell, *Trucks Roll!* by George Ella Lyon, and *Trucks, Trucks, Trucks* by Peter Sis.

• Invite children to create their own "teaching" books about their main areas of interest. Encourage them to draw and add labels as best they can.

• Continue to support the children's areas of interest with related field trips, Internet exploration, and conversations with experts.

Look Who's Learning to Read

# 5. Rhyming Read-Alouds

*ACCOMPLISHMENTS: recognizing rhyming words, creating original rhymes, listening to read-alouds*

It's no surprise that so many picture books for young children are written in rhyme. After all, children love to hear, repeat, and memorize rhymes. Attending to the sounds of rhymes also supports the beginning reader. Children learn to recognize rhyming words, substitute initial sounds, and add or delete sounds to create rhyming words. Above all, children learn to appreciate the meaning in yet another good story. This activity is appropriate for all children aged 2 to 5.

## MATERIALS TO GATHER

All that is required for this essential read-aloud activity is one appealing picture book that contains rhyming text. Here, Rick Walton's *Bunnies on the Go: Getting From Place to Place* is shared. Browse books listed in the Appendix under Favorite Read-Alouds to discover many other rhyming texts. The format of the invitation below can be used for most rhyming picture books.

## INVITATIONS TO PLAY

◆ Introduce the book by sharing the front cover and title. Share the name of the author and illustrator with children aged 2½ and up.

> This book is called *Bunnies on the Go: Getting From Place to Place*.
>
> An author named Rick Walton wrote this story. He had the idea for the story and he chose just the right words to tell the story well. A woman named Paige Miglio drew the beautiful pictures to go with Rick's words. She's called the illustrator. Her illustrations help us understand the story. She drew the bunny family on the cover, traveling in a red car.

◆ If children are articulate enough to engage in conversation, you might ask a probing question.

> What do you think we might learn about this bunny family when we open the book?

◆ Be accepting of children's answers if they make sense. If answers do not make sense, remind children about the title and subtitle.

> Well, let's read and find out.

◆ Read the entire text through, following read-aloud suggestions on pages 10–12.

◆ Be sure to talk about illustrations, answer children's questions about each mode of transportation, respond to their comments, help them connect personally to the different ways of travel, and discuss the meaning of the ending. (The illustrations in this book are particularly intriguing, as the illustrator tucks in a preview of the next vehicle on every two-page spread.)

◆ Reread the book aloud, this time pausing just slightly in order to invite the children to chime in with the name of the rhyming mode of transportation. (In this book, the rhyming word at the end of each four-line stanza appears after you turn the page. This layout makes it particularly easy to encourage children to call out the upcoming rhyming words.)

## TIPS TO CONSIDER

◆ It is particularly helpful to rehearse your reading of rhyming texts to be sure that you know how to read it aloud well. Rehearsing will make it easier for you to accentuate the correct words and pause in just the right places so that the children can fill in the upcoming rhyming words.

◆ Always encourage children to study the illustrations. Show your admiration when they notice details in them.

◆ Be sure to attend to the meaning of the book as a whole and not simply to the sound of rhyming words.

### POSSIBILITIES TO EXTEND THE LEARNING

• After rereading and discussing the book and the illustrations, you might play with the rhyming words. Say the key word, asking children to think of a rhyming means of transportation (*far/car, lane/train, dragon/wagon*, etc). It is not necessary to define rhyming for children. Explain the meaning of the word by offering examples.

• Revisit Follow Their Lead on page 13, as *Each Peach Pear Plum* is also a rhyming text.

• Share many other rhyming texts, asking librarians for suggestions. Also consult Favorite Read-Alouds in the Appendix, selecting books that rhyme.

# 6. Hide-and-Seek With Books

*ACCOMPLISHMENTS: learning opposites, following directions, listening to read-alouds*

This hide-and-seek activity combines learning the meaning of opposites, following directions, finding hidden book treasures, and listening to books read aloud after locating them. It is appropriate for children aged 2½ and up.

## MATERIALS TO GATHER

This activity simply requires a favorite book or a new one from the library and a room in which to play hide-and-seek with the chosen book. As children search for the hidden book, you will need to help them by offering hints through the use of opposites. Several helpful opposites appear in the invitations below.

## INVITATIONS TO PLAY

◆ Hide a favorite children's book or a new one from the library in an easily accessible place, one that is safely within reach of the children.

> You know how we sometimes play hide-and-seek. You close your eyes and count to ten and I hide and then you try to find me. And sometimes you hide and I try to find you. Well, today we are going to play a different kind of hide-and-seek. Are you ready?
>
> When we returned from the library, I took one of the books we borrowed and I hid it in this room. Now we can play hide-and-seek with that book.
>
> You can try and find it, and I will give you hints. I will tell you how you are doing and make suggestions to help you find the book.
>
> If you are close to the book, I will say you are hot.
>
> If you are far away, I will say you are cold.
>
> If you move toward the book, I will say you are getting hotter.
>
> If you move away, I will say you are getting colder.

◆ In addition to the opposites of hot and cold, try to weave in opposites in other hints. A few examples follow:

> Look *up*—don't look *down*.
>
> You are *near* now—you're not *far*.
>
> It's not *inside* anything—it's *outside*.
>
> It's not on something *smooth*—it's on something *rough*.
>
> Don't look to the *left*—look to the *right*.
>
> Don't look *over* the table—look *under* it.
>
> It's not in *back* of the bookcase—it's in *front* of it.
>
> Look *higher*—don't look *lower*.
>
> You're getting *closer*—you're not moving *farther* away.
>
> *Slow down*—don't *rush* when you search.
>
> It's behind something very *old*—not something *new*.

◆ Of course, stop to read and enjoy the book when it is found. That's the grand reward!

◆ Continue hiding other books if children remain interested.

## TIPS TO CONSIDER

◆ Make it fairly easy for very young children to find the books, so as not to frustrate them.

◆ Make sure that hiding spots do not require unsafe climbing or lifting.

◆ Explain the meaning of unfamiliar opposites. (Young children may not know the difference between left and right.)

◆ Be sure to read the book aloud when it's found, building in reading aloud as an essential part of the game.

### POSSIBILITIES TO EXTEND THE LEARNING

• When children are ready, ask *them* to hide the books and give *you* clues. Children might begin with just saying hot or cold as you move about the room, searching for the hidden book.

• Borrow picture books about opposites from the library, including *Over Under* by Marthe Jocelyn, *Big Fish Little Fish* by Ed Heck, and *Yummy Yucky, Big Little,* and *Quiet Loud* by Leslie Patricelli.

• Arrange four or five familiar books on a low table, with front covers visible. Review the titles with children. Ask children to close their eyes as you remove one of the books. Children have to guess which one was taken. After children guess, continue playing by hiding a different book. Reverse roles, asking children to hide books, so you can guess which is missing. As always, end the activity by reading the books aloud.

# RETELLING STORIES

## 7. Book Path Journey

*ACCOMPLISHMENTS: recognizing titles and covers, retelling stories*

In this active indoor game, children are invited to walk on a path created by books they know and love. This activity combines recalling book titles, story plots and cover illustrations with physical activity and strategic thinking. It is appropriate for children aged 2½ to 6.

## MATERIALS TO GATHER

Spread your children's frequently read books out on the floor, creating a winding path (see photograph at right). You can include library books, homemade books, and any books the children own. The important element is that the books are familiar to the child. You can create a simple path with as few as five to ten books or create more complicated, winding paths with a larger collection. Be sure the titles are facing up, making it easier for the children to spot them.

## INVITATIONS TO PLAY

◆ Show children how to line up books to create a path. Then present the following game.

> I've made a path of your favorite books. Would you like to learn a new game using this path of books?
>
> Please stand right here on the first one at the bottom of this path and I will challenge you to find others.

◆ Pose questions such as the following:

> Can you find a book about a man who wants to sell hats but whose hats are stolen by monkeys when he takes a rest? (*Caps for Sale* by Esphyr Slobodkina)
>
> Can you find a book about a little teddy bear who loses his button in a department store? (*Corduroy* by Don Freeman)
>
> Can you find a book about a missing sheep? (*Where Is the Green Sheep?* by Mem Fox)

◆ Continue to play as long as children are interested.

## TIPS TO CONSIDER

◆ To avoid their slipping on books, make sure children remove shoes and wear socks with rubber grips on the bottom. Use hardcover books rather than paperbacks, and encourage slow walking, not running.

◆ Remind children to stay on the path—no walking across the floor or the rug. Part of the fun is in figuring out how you will get to the book described.

◆ If children can't spot the book, offer clues. For example, you might say something like "It's right under the book about the three little pigs" or "It's at the top of the first column near the radiator."

◆ If children can't remember the book, offer clues. For example, you might say something like "That book has a picture on the cover of a mommy bunny taking care of her ten little bunnies." Be sure to reread the forgotten books aloud to the children at a later time.

## POSSIBILITIES TO EXTEND THE LEARNING

• Modify the instructions, substituting words for *find*. Say instead, "Can you *search for / scrounge around for / hunt for / try to locate* . . ." Children's vocabulary will grow when you naturally weave in words with a similar meaning. (See New Words Naturally, page 92.)

• Invite children who can retell story plots to switch roles with you. The children give the clues and you find the books.

• Invite children to select the books and create the path.

• Change books as more books become familiar to the children.

# 8. Board Book Building

*ACCOMPLISHMENTS: recalling story titles and characters, inspiring rereading*

This activity satisfies the toddler's urge to build roads, bridges, tunnels, and mazes for their toy vehicles as well as to construct towers. Using board books as building materials helps youngsters recall familiar books and inspires rereading. It is appropriate for children aged 2½ and up.

## MATERIALS TO GATHER

This game requires as many board books as possible but can be played with as few as ten. (Board books are those thick-paged books intended for toddlers. Their pages are made from thick cardboard to minimize tearing.) Borrow as many from your public library as is permissible. Gather them in your home and/or invite neighborhood children over to pool your resources.

Read books to children several times before using them for constructions.

## INVITATIONS TO PLAY

◆ Introduce activity.

These books with very thick pages are called board books. Today, instead of just reading them, we are going to use them to make all kinds of buildings. Let's start with a tower. Do you think we can stack all of these up so carefully that they don't fall down?

◆ Hand books to the children with the front covers facing up and with the spines facing the same direction so that you can read the titles. Also, hand larger books to the children first to facilitate the balancing required.

Let's count how many floors (levels, stories) are in our tower.

Right, there are ten. Let's pretend that each book is a family living in our tower. Let's see who lives on the top floor.

◆ Share the title and offer to read the book aloud. Return book to the top of the tower.

Can you tell who lives on the bottom floor?

◆ Encourage children to look at the spines of the books to figure out which book "family" lives on the bottom floor of the tower. Carefully slip out the book and read it aloud. Slip it back when you are done so that the tower continues to have ten floors.

◆ Continue asking children which book families live on the other floors.

Yes, the *Goodnight Moon* bunny family lives on the sixth floor.

Yes, the very hungry caterpillar lives on the third floor.

Yes, the boy who planted the carrot seed lives on the eighth floor.

◆ Continue offering to read books aloud.

Perhaps we can use our board books to build a bridge. How should we do that?

◆ If children need assistance, you can help them create two short stacks a short distance apart from one another with a larger board book balanced over the top of both stacks, creating a bridge. See photograph at right.

Would you like to send your toy cars and trucks across this bridge?

Maybe we should call our bridge the Good Night, Gorilla, Bridge because that is the name of the book that is spanning our stacks.

Perhaps we can use our board books differently now and create a tunnel. Do you have any ideas on how to do that?

◆ If necessary, you can show children how board books can be placed to form a tent-like structure. (Spines face the ceiling; pages face the floor. The open center page will support the book to make the tent shape, an upside-down V.) Line books up touching one another in a straight line, forming a tunnel. (See photograph at right.)

Now let's see if your cars can make it through the tunnel.

◆ Sit at one end of the tunnel, with children at the other. Encourage children to roll the vehicle into the book tunnel so you can send it back. If the vehicle does not make it out of the tunnel, you can ask children, "Look in the tunnel. Which book do you think we have to lift to get your car back?"

◆ Offer to read books aloud whenever they are lifted from the tunnel formation.

I think it's time for a book break.

## TIPS TO CONSIDER

◆ If children have trouble stacking books, you can prop up the tower against a wall.

◆ If children are slow at building because they stop to browse books, simply rejoice in their interest.

◆ If you use the word *stories* to refer to the number of floors in a building, take the occasion to explain that some words—homonyms—sound alike and are spelled alike but have different meanings. There can be many stories in a fairy tale collection and many stories in a skyscraper.

## POSSIBILITIES TO EXTEND THE LEARNING

- You can also initiate a "Touch That Book!" ball game. Stand up ten familiar board books next to one another across the room, so that children can easily see all covers. Children sit a few feet away from the books with a rubber ball for rolling. Children announce the title of the book they are hoping to touch with the ball. If they touch the book, remove it from the lineup and read it aloud. The game is over when children have touched and heard all the books.

- Book mazes require more than ten board books and a large floor space. If you can gather a stack of at least 20 books, you can create a maze for children, showing them where to enter and how to walk through until they find their way out. Use the books to build the "walls" of the maze. Stand books up by spreading the pages out and then arrange them in paths that twist and turn. (See photograph at right.) Eventually children will want to design their own book mazes. Expect the books to fall down occasionally and expect children to stop and read as they work.

# 9. Familiar Phrases

*ACCOMPLISHMENTS: learning literary language, recalling stories*

Children's stories are filled with refrains, lines that are repeated throughout the story. Classic fairy tales are particularly rich in these memorable lines. In this activity, these literary lines are used in everyday conversations. This practice helps children delight in literary language and recall favorite stories. This activity is appropriate for all children who are familiar with the stories containing these lines.

## MATERIALS TO GATHER

Read and reread aloud such classic children's stories as "The Gingerbread Man," "The Three Billy Goats Gruff," "The Three Little Pigs," "Snow White and the Seven Dwarfs," "Little Red Riding Hood," "The Little Red Hen," and "Chicken Little." Any version will do; in fact, read several versions of each. Retellings of these stories also often appear as part of children's television programming and can be borrowed from most public libraries in audio CD and DVD formats. Learn these stories well enough so that you can even tell them without the aid of the printed text.

## INVITATIONS TO PLAY

◆ Whenever appropriate, weave these lines into everyday conversations. For example, if children are familiar with "The Gingerbread Man," you could exclaim when you are playing in the park or backyard, "Run, run as fast as you can. You can't catch me, I'm the _____." Encourage children to fill in the missing word.

If children are familiar with "The Three Billy Goats Gruff," you could ask, "Who's that trip-trapping across my bridge?" whenever someone is making an unusual noise.

If children are familiar with "The Three Little Pigs," you could announce, "Little pig, little pig, let me come in," when children are behind closed doors. Encourage children to answer, "Not by the hair on my chinny-chin-chin."

If children are familiar with "The Little Red Hen," you could ask, "Who will help me?" whenever there is a chore to be done. Encourage children to respond, " 'Not I,' said the goose. 'Not I,' said the pig. 'Not I,' said the cat." Of course, encourage them to add, "But I will help you!"

If children are familiar with "Chicken Little," you could call out, "Oh no, the sky is falling!" whenever children watch snowflakes fly about in a windstorm or confetti float at a celebration.

If children are familiar with "Little Red Riding Hood," you could comment, "What big eyes you have!" whenever you are washing their faces. Encourage children to respond, "Better to see you with." Do likewise with "What big ears you have!" encouraging children to respond, "Better to hear you with!"

If children are familiar with "Snow White," you could ask, "Mirror, mirror on the wall, who's the fairest (bravest/kindest/tallest) one of all?" whenever children are looking in a mirror.

◆ Each time you refer to a literary line, you could ask children if they recall which book it comes from.

Do you remember which book that line is from?

Do you think we can locate that book?

Let's reread that book.

## TIPS TO CONSIDER

◆ Be sure to celebrate whenever children use literary language on their own. For example, when they begin a story with "Once upon a time" or end one with "And they lived happily ever after," they are borrowing from literature. That's cause for celebration.

◆ Reread stories as often as possible. Children become better readers, writers, and storytellers when they know stories by heart.

◆ Don't hesitate to vary or personalize refrains, substituting children's names. For example, "Ben, Ben, let me come in."

## POSSIBILITIES TO EXTEND THE LEARNING

• Fairy tales aren't the only stories that contain refrains, or distinctive lines that are memorable. Don't hesitate to include these as well in your everyday conversations. For example, if your children adore Watty Piper's *The Little Engine That Could*, you could chant, "I think I can, I think I can, I think I can" whenever you are attempting a difficult task. Encourage children to do likewise.

• Read other classic stories, searching for refrains to weave into everyday conversations.

# STORYTELLING

# 10. Can't Stump Me

*ACCOMPLISHMENTS: retelling stories, recognizing story elements*

Being familiar with many stories, understanding how these stories work (their structures), and being able to retell stories are important parts of becoming a successful reader. In this literary guessing game, children are asked to figure out the name of a fairy tale, fable, picture book, or even nursery rhyme after hearing several general statements about the plot. Children are then invited to offer the clues and ask an adult to guess the source. This activity is appropriate for children aged 3 and up.

## MATERIALS TO GATHER

This activity requires that children and their caregivers or teachers are familiar with several fairy tales, fables, picture books, and/or nursery rhymes. The names of many classic ones appear in Possibilities to Extend the Learning.

## INVITATIONS TO PLAY

◆ Children are creatures of habit and seem to delight in predictable routines and family rituals. Try playing Can't Stump Me each morning as you prepare breakfast, each night as you dry children after their baths, or as part of children's bedtime rituals. At school, play the game when children line up for dismissal or await the arrival of a guest speaker.

Before you close your eyes tonight, I am going to tell you two stories, but I am going to tell them in a very special way. I am going to give you hints about the stories, and you will have to guess which stories I am talking about.

Let's see if I can really stump you. That means you're not going to be able to guess what story I am talking about. Are you ready?

◆ Tell the first story in rather general terms, omitting character names and other specific details that would give the title away too quickly.

Once there was a little girl who had a family member, a relative, she was told to visit. She decided to bring some treats for this family member. So she got dressed in her usual favorite outfit in her usual favorite color and set out on her journey. Unfortunately, along the way she stopped to talk to a creature who wasn't very nice and he set out to ruin her plans. He pretended to be her family member and hurt this little girl. Luckily, someone came by and saved the little girl and her family member.

◆ If children don't recognize this bare-bones retelling of "Little Red Riding Hood," offer a few more specific hints.

> Well, this little girl just loved the color red.
>
> And this little girl went to visit her grandmother.
>
> And this creature, a bad wolf, pretended to be her grandmother.
>
> And the little girl knew that her grandmother looked different because her eyes and her teeth weren't as big as the creature's.

◆ When children guess correctly, announce, "Well, I couldn't stump you!"

◆ Tell one more before the children go to sleep.

> Let's see if I can stump you this time . . .
>
> There once was a young woman who had to work very hard in her house because some members of her family weren't very nice to her. She spent all day doing chores. One day there was a big party in town and her family members were going, but they said she couldn't go because she had too much work to do and no pretty outfit to wear. Then something magical happened and the woman was able to go to the party, but she had to leave early. When she was leaving, she dropped something important because she was rushing to get home. The next day the host of the party came looking for the person who lost the important thing. Unfortunately, her family locked her up so the host couldn't meet her. But fortunately, a little tiny creature helped the young woman get free so the visitor could see her and find out that she was the person at the party who lost that important thing. And the two of them lived happily ever after.

◆ If children don't recognize this bare-bones retelling of "Cinderella," offer a few more specific hints.

> Yes, she had so many chores, including wiping the cinders from the fireplace.
>
> Her stepmother and stepsisters weren't very nice to her.
>
> The party was a grand ball, given by a prince.
>
> Her fairy godmother made it possible for her to attend.
>
> Too bad she dropped her shoe. It was a glass slipper.

◆ When children guess correctly, announce, "Well, I couldn't stump you tonight, but I'll try again tomorrow night."

## TIPS TO CONSIDER

◆ When offering your clues, try to find the right balance between general and specific. In other words, avoid details that are too specific, as they will take away the challenge. But include the gist of the story so that the children can be successful.

◆ If children have trouble identifying the stories, spend time rereading a few of them and retelling them throughout the day. Refer to the same ones at bedtime until children recognize them easily. Add more specific clues as needed.

◆ If children are interested in having a turn but are not quite ready to prepare a retelling on their own, encourage them to reuse the tale you have selected, repeating your general statements.

◆ When children are ready to retell a story on their own, be accepting of their attempts even if their retellings are too general and therefore impossible to identify or too specific and therefore rather obvious. Be proud of all their attempts, as retelling in general terms is quite challenging.

## POSSIBILITIES TO EXTEND THE LEARNING

• Other traditional stories to use in this activity include "The Three Billy Goats Gruff," "The Three Little Pigs," "Henny Penny," "The Little Red Hen," "The Gingerbread Boy," "Pinocchio," "Hansel and Gretel," "The Boy Who Cried Wolf," and "Jack and the Beanstalk."

• Borrow fairy tale anthologies from the public library. Read them aloud to children or retell the classics from memory. Once children are familiar with new stories, include them in your Can't Stump Me repertoire.

• In addition to anthologies, ask your public librarian for picture book versions of any classic stories by such writers as Hans Christian Andersen, the Brothers Grimm, and Aesop. Include these stories when you play Can't Stump Me.

• Children can also become familiar with classic stories by watching video, cartoon, or puppet show versions.

• Don't hesitate to refer to any picture book or nursery rhyme that the children enjoy. In other words, you need not use only traditional ones. For example, you could retell the plot of *Caps for Sale* or even "Jack and Jill" in very general terms.

• Read aloud *Once Upon a Time, the End (Asleep in 60 Seconds)* by Geoffrey Kloske. Ask children to talk about which parts of these condensed classic stories are missing.

Look Who's Learning to Read

# 11. Party Favor Storytelling

*ACCOMPLISHMENTS: learning the conventions of story, telling stories*

Children take part in this storytelling activity by prompting the adult storyteller with small toys found in the home. In time, children take on the role of storyteller, learning the conventions of story. They come to understand the importance of having inviting beginnings, engaging and sustaining middles, and satisfying endings. In addition to hearing lots and lots of quickly developed stories, children delight in putting their party favors to good use. This activity is appropriate for all ages.

## MATERIALS TO GATHER

This activity requires acquiring an empty clear-plastic jug, the kind that pretzels, licorice, nuts, or cookies are often sold in. Next, comes the search for random miniature toys. These toys are often given out as party favors, offered as gifts in fast food restaurants, or tucked into cereal or Cracker Jack boxes. They include small figurines, vehicles, noisemakers, birthday cake decorations, key chains, bubble wands, plastic charms and whistles. Fill the jug with the toys gathered and delight in putting these objects to a brand-new use. Continue adding to this collection whenever these small, seemingly useless toys are brought home. Teachers can ask children to bring such items to class.

## INVITATIONS TO PLAY

- Introduce the activity.

    I have something very surprising to show you. This morning I walked around the house collecting lots of little toys. They are so small that each can fit into your pocket. I put them all into this empty jug, the one that used to have pretzels in it. Can you see all of them in there?

- Invite children to call out the names of the objects they see.

- Then invite children to feel around for others.

    There are many more that you can't see.

    They are hidden behind the others.

    Put your hand in and pull one out.

- Make sure that children are familiar with all the objects.

    Let's pour them out so you can see them all.

- Introduce the storytelling activity.

    Now I am going to teach you a new game using these little objects. I want you to select two, and then I will make up a story using these two items.

    If there are two children present, ask each of them to pick one object. Then make up a story with the two selections.

    Oh my goodness, you've chosen a tiny plastic octopus and a miniature American flag. Let me think now, how can I create a story around those two items?

◆ Have fun creating a short story—the sillier the better for most young children.

Once upon a time there was a very shy octopus. He lived by himself at the bottom of the Hudson River. He was very shy and didn't make new friends very easily.

One day, the shy octopus thought to himself, "If only I had something exciting to talk about, then I would make new friends easily."

So the shy octopus thought and thought. "What exciting thing can I do?" he wondered.

He tried to climb the biggest mountain, but that didn't work—his eight tentacles got in the way.

He tried to build the tallest building, but that didn't work—his eight tentacles got in the way.

He tried to jump with the world's longest jump rope, but that didn't work—his eight tentacles got in the way.

So the shy octopus thought some more.

"I've got it!" said the shy octopus to himself. "I will fly a rocket ship to the moon! Then I will have something really exciting to talk about."

So he tried to fly a rocket ship to the moon, and guess what? His eight tentacles didn't get in the way. No, they didn't get in the way at all. In fact, he needed all eight of them because he had to press three buttons, lift three levers, and pull two handles—all at the same time!

And when the shy octopus landed on the moon, he proudly held up an American flag and announced, "Hello, everybody on Earth. It's me, your friend the octopus, who lives at the bottom of the Hudson River. I'll be flying home soon. Please come and visit me."

And the shy octopus was never shy again. He was so happy to talk about his trip to the moon. He was so happy to talk about how handy it is to have eight tentacles. He was so happy to have visitors at the bottom of the Hudson River that he lived happily ever after.

◆ Ask children to select another two objects and continue making up stories as long as they seem interested.

## TIPS TO CONSIDER

◆ If you are new to creating original stories, refer to the following guidelines until you are ready to go it alone.
  • Try beginning with lines like "Once upon a time" and ending with lines like "And they lived happily ever after."
  • Be sure to anchor your story in a particular time and location (setting).
  • Create characters that children will care about.
  • Give background information and then shift to "One day . . ."
  • Create a problem that needs to be solved.
  • Include several unsuccessful attempts at solving the problem before discovering a successful one.
  • Use repetition if appropriate. ("He tried___, but that didn't work—his eight tentacles got in the way.")

## POSSIBILITIES TO EXTEND THE LEARNING

- If children seem ready and interested, switch roles. You select the objects and children make up the stories.

- If a story seems particularly engaging, write it down so you can read it to children at another time.

- Play a similar game using a picture dictionary. Ask a child to open to any page and point to an item. Then ask her (or another child) to open to another page, selecting a second item. Use both selections to tell a story.

- Judy Mulford, a renowned California artist and basket weaver, played another storytelling game with her two grandsons. Each was asked to whisper a word in Judy's ear. She then had to create a story using their selections.

- Create a four-page booklet by stapling pages together or folding a large sheet into a four-page booklet. Ask children to pick four stickers from their collections, placing one on each page. "Read" the book to the children by making up a story that connects the four stickers. Invite the children to do likewise by choosing four more stickers and placing them on pages in a booklet.

- If any characters become particularly engaging to children, refer to them apart from this activity. Let them take on a life of their own, inviting children to delight in stories in a series. (For example, the shy octopus can become a recurring character in other stories you tell). Then too, you can get children hooked on a series borrowed from the public library. Popular series include the following:

    Katharine Holabird's Angelina Ballerina books
    Lauren Thompson's  Mouse's First . . . books
    Ian Falconer's Olivia books
    Lauren Thompson's Little Quack books
    Rosemary Wells's Max and Ruby books
    Eric Hill's Spot books
    Jonathan London's Froggy books
    Nancy White Carlstrom's Jesse Bear books
    Mick Inkpen's Wibbly Pig books
    Marc Brown's Arthur books
    Janet Morgan Stoeke's Minerva Louise books
    Karma Wilson's Bear books
    Margret and H. A. Rey's Curious George books
    Norman Bridwell's Clifford books

# 12. Silly Story Fill-Ins

*ACCOMPLISHMENTS: learning initial consonant sounds, learning to make meaningful guesses, using context clues, telling stories*

This activity requires you to make up very simple short stories for the children in your care. At crucial moments you pause, omit a word that begins with a consonant, and ask the children to help complete the story. Remind children that the words they choose must make sense, although they delight when the suggestions are silly ones. By offering initial-consonant clues (the first letter in words), you invite children to connect alphabet letters with the sounds they make (sound-symbol correspondence). Children also learn what it means to tell a story. This activity is appropriate for children aged 3 and up.

## MATERIALS TO GATHER

No materials are required for this activity, although if you are not used to making up stories for children, you may want to prepare a few in advance. The stories below will give you ideas as to how to frame the missing words.

## INVITATIONS TO PLAY

◆ Children love to hear stories throughout the day. Stories come in especially handy when you need to distract children, shift them to a new activity, make long waits bearable, and, of course, put them to bed. Make sure to pick topics that are familiar to your children, as that will make it easier for them to become involved in the story. The first story below is about soccer and the second is about being a flower girl at a wedding. The stories become interactive when the teller pauses at missing words, just providing the sound that the initial letter makes.

◆ Offer to share a story with children.

Once upon a time, a little boy named Ben was getting ready to play soccer. His mother said, "Don't forget, when you play soccer, on your feet you must wear s____. (*Just make the /s/ sound, sort of a "ssss" sound.*)

I wonder what his mom told him to wear. It starts with the letter *s*. It begins with the /s/ sound. Let's see, how about sand castles?

Do you think his mom wants him to wear sand castles on his feet when he plays soccer?

◆ Encourage children to respond.

No, you're right—that's too silly. You can't wear sand castles.

How about sandwiches?

You're right. That's also silly and too messy.

How about scissors?

You're correct. That's ridiculous as well and too dangerous.

I know, how about sunglasses?

No, that's wrong. You can't wear sunglasses on your feet.

◆ If they don't respond, keep thinking aloud.

Let me think now—on his feet? Sssss. Hmmmm! How about slippers? No, you can't play soccer in slippers. How about sandals? No, you can't kick a ball well in sandals.

◆ If children suggest shoes, congratulate them for making such a meaningful and sensible choice. It would be too complicated to explain that even though shoes starts with the letter *s*, it makes a special sound because the *s* is combined with the *h*. You might respond as follows:

That's right. It makes sense for his mom to say, "Don't forget to wear shoes on your feet when you play soccer." In fact, I think she wants him to wear a very special kind of shoe when he plays soccer, one that begins with the /s/ sound.

◆ Encourage children to guess again.

I've got it! His mom wants him to wear sneakers! That makes the most sense.

◆ Remember to finish the story, so it sounds complete.

So Ben put on his sneakers and he kicked the soccer ball so well that his team won the game. And all the players went to Ben's house to celebrate. They drank lemonade and ate chocolate chip cookies, and everyone congratulated Ben for being such a good player. That night, Ben dreamed of being a super soccer star!

◆ Here's another sample story.

Once upon a time, a little girl named Andie was asked to be a flower girl in a wedding. Her mother told her that when she walked down the aisle she would carry a basket filled with beautiful and colorful things to gently scatter onto the ground. So Andie put on a very fancy dress and went to the wedding. She had to wait for the music to start and then she had to slowly walk down the aisle and make a glorious path for the bride. The music finally began. Andie lifted her basket and began to walk. And as she walked, she gently scattered p____. (*Just make a /p/, or "puh," sound.*)

I wonder what was in the basket.

◆ Offer silly choices to entertain the children.

Maybe pretzels? No, that wouldn't make a beautiful path for the bride.

How about peanuts? No, that would make a lumpy, crunchy path.

Perhaps pickles? No, that would make the wedding smell like pickles!

◆ Encourage the children to guess, reminding them that the missing word starts with the letter *p* and makes the /p/, or "puh," sound.

Wait a minute. She was a flower girl. I've got it. There were petals in the basket. She scattered beautiful and colorful petals.

(If children are familiar with the precise names of flowers or seem ready to learn about them, you could suggest that petunias and pansies are in the basket as well.)

◆ Be sure to end the story.

So Andie scattered beautiful and colorful petals all down the aisle. She scattered red petals. She scattered pink petals. She scattered yellow petals.

And she made a glorious path for the bride. And everyone was so proud of Andie the flower girl that they gave her a beautiful bouquet to take home. And all the family lived happily ever after.

## TIPS TO CONSIDER

◆ It is best to omit words that begin with consonants, as vowels often have many sounds.

◆ It is best to omit nouns at the end of sentences. The names of objects work especially well.
    On your feet, you must wear s_____.
    As she walked she scattered p_____.

◆ The story about Ben is a very simple one. The story about Andie has more literary qualities, like books found in the library. When you tell stories, consider using such conventions of story as "Once upon a time" and "They lived happily ever after." Choose interesting words, as in "She made a *glorious* path" and "She *scattered* the petals." You can also use literary repetition, as in: "She scattered red petals. She scattered pink petals. She scattered yellow petals."

◆ Be sure to complete each story so children learn that stories should have a satisfying ending and feel complete.

◆ If children are not ready to guess possible words connected to the sound of the initial letter, simply provide choices yourself. Trust that in time they will begin to understand how your choices are dictated by the sound of the first letter of the word.

◆ Whenever children offer guesses, be sure to comment on whether the guess makes sense. When young children learn to read, they often guess at words, and this strategy is effective if children are making meaningful, sensible guesses.

## POSSIBILITIES TO EXTEND THE LEARNING

• When rereading picture books aloud to children, you can occasionally pause at a word and ask children to guess what probably comes next. If they are listening for meaning, they will be able to offer an appropriate word. For example, in the classic book *The Carrot Seed* by Ruth Krauss, you can leave off the last word, telling children that the youngster planted a carrot s_____ (make the /s/ sound). Respond to children's guesses. For example, if children guess *sandwich*, you might say the following:
    Yes *sandwich* begins with the right sound, but does *sandwich* make sense? Would you plant a carrot sandwich? What might we plant? Yes, seeds.

• You can do likewise when you read aloud the part about the child sprinkling the ground with w_____ (make the /w/ sound).
    Yes, he had to water the plants so they could grow. He sprinkled the ground with water.

# DEEPENING READING COMPREHENSION

# 13. Toys and Texts

*ACCOMPLISHMENTS: taking on points of view, listening to read-alouds*

This activity invites youngsters to play with their favorite animal toys as well as their books. Very young readers-to-be are simply asked to match the toy with a topic-related book. Older children are asked to take on different points of view, an essential reading comprehension skill that can be introduced in a most gentle way at an early age. Read-alouds are appropriate for all ages, probing questions for children aged 3½ and up.

## MATERIALS TO GATHER

Gather children's favorite animal toys. Then look for books that match the toys. Here, a sheep figurine is paired with Mem Fox's *Where Is the Green Sheep?*, a mouse puppet with Lucy Cousins's *Maisy Takes a Bath*, a stuffed penguin with Mary Murphy's *I Like It When . . .* , a wind-up dog with Eric Hill's *Spot's Treasure Hunt*, and a teddy bear with Don Freeman's *Corduroy*. Spread the books out on a low table and place the toys in a basket alongside them.

## INVITATIONS TO PLAY

◆ Introduce the activity.
   Today, before I read to you, I am going to ask you to look at this basket of toys. I picked a perfect toy for you to hold while I read each book. Look through this basket and decide which toy would make sense to hold while I read *Where Is the Green Sheep?*

◆ Ask children to place the toy on top of the book.
   Of course, you chose the sheep because this book is about a missing green sheep.

◆ Ask children to continue selecting toys to accompany each remaining book.
   Which one would be a good match for *Maisy*? How about *I Like It When . . .*? And *Spot*? That leaves *Corduroy*.

◆ If books are unfamiliar to children, suggest that they use the illustrations as clues.
   This is a book you haven't heard before, but the picture on the cover will give you a hint.

◆ When all books and toys are paired, offer to read the books aloud.
   Which book should I read aloud first? You can hold the matching toy as I read.

◆ With older children or those who are ready, you can ask probing questions after the read-aloud.
   How do you think this toy sheep would feel if he could hear this story? What might he say or do?

◆ Be accepting of children's responses. If there are responses, offer your own.

I think this sheep might feel bad that the green sheep is missing. Maybe he would say, "Let's look everywhere." Maybe he would search all over the neighborhood for the green sheep.

How do you think this toy penguin would feel if he could hear *I Like It When . . .*? What might he say? What might he do?

◆ Again, invite children to respond and be accepting of children's responses.

◆ If there are no responses, offer your own.

I think this toy penguin would feel happy for the baby penguin because he does so many things with his mother. Maybe he would say, "I like to eat new things and dance to music, too." Maybe he would want to visit that penguin family's house.

◆ Add similar questions to go along with the books about Maisy, Corduroy, and Spot.

## TIPS TO CONSIDER

◆ Follow read-aloud tips on pages 10–12.

◆ If young children have trouble matching toys to books, you may want to read books aloud first and then ask children to connect toy to topic.

◆ Young children have varying attention spans for listening to stories read aloud. You may be able to read only one or two books at a sitting.

◆ Some children may choose to play with the toys instead of listening to the read-aloud. If so, save the read-aloud for later.

## POSSIBILITIES TO EXTEND THE LEARNING

• Use toys for dramatic play, asking children to act out familiar stories.

• Ask children to choose other animal toys as well as dolls that they would like to match with books. Search in the library for titles that connect with toys. You might make choices such as the following:

*Angelina Ballerina* by Katharine Holabird—toy mouse or ballerina doll

*Curious George* by H. A. Rey—toy monkey

*Firefighter Frank* by Monica Wellington—firefighter doll

*Goodnight Moon* by Margaret Wise Brown—toy bunny

*Harry the Dirty Dog* by Gene Zion—toy dog

*Leo the Late Bloomer* by Robert Kraus—toy tiger

*The Story of Babar the Little Elephant* by Jean de Brunhoff—toy elephant

*Winnie-the-Pooh* by A. A. Milne—stuffed teddy bear

# 14. Reading Faces, Reading Books

*ACCOMPLISHMENTS: listening to and responding to stories, empathizing with characters*

Being able to read people's emotions and moods and then respond appropriately and with empathy is just as important in life as being able to read best sellers, the daily mail, or your local newspaper. This activity asks youngsters to read children's expressions on the covers of picture books and then listen to and respond to their stories. It is appropriate for children aged 2½ and up.

## MATERIALS TO GATHER

Browse public library shelves, classroom bookcases or children's bedroom collections for books that have expressive faces on their covers. Choose ones with children making faces and gestures that show such emotions and moods as happy, sad, scared, proud, disappointed, angry, embarrassed, or surprised.

## INVITATIONS TO PLAY

◆ Spread out the collection of books, inviting children to see faces on the covers.

Here are three books I borrowed from the library today. Look at all these children on the covers.

Which child looks happy to you?

Yes, this boy on the cover of *Pete's a Pizza* sure looks happy.

Which child looks sad?

Yes, this boy on the cover of *Alexander and the Terrible, Horrible, No Good, Very Bad Day* looks very sad.

Which child looks scared to you?

Yes, this child on the cover of *What Do You Do When a Monster Says Boo?* certainly looks scared.

I wonder why that boy is happy, that one is sad, and that one is scared. Should we read and find out? Which one should we read first?

◆ Let children choose order of books to read aloud.

◆ With older children, before reading the books, you might ask:

Why might that boy be happy? What makes you happy?

Why might that boy be sad? What makes you sad?

Why might that boy be scared? What makes you scared?

◆ After reading the books aloud, study the covers once again, recalling why the children felt the way they did.

So this boy was happy because his daddy played with him, pretending to make pizza out of him. But remember, at first he was sad because he wanted to play ball and it started to rain. He sure was happy when the sun came out.

And this boy was sad because so many things went wrong for him all in one day. Some days are like that.

And this boy was scared because his sister pretended to be a monster.

Let's look through this shelf of books and see if there are any others that have happy children on the cover, or sad ones, or scared-looking ones.

## TIPS TO CONSIDER

◆ Follow read-aloud tips on pages 10–12.

◆ Ask a librarian to help you find high-quality books with expressive children's faces on their covers. These might include *When Sophie Gets Angry . . . Really, Really Angry* by Molly Bang or *Walter Was Worried* by Laura Vaccaro Seeger.

◆ Children may not be able to tell the difference between a face that looks proud and one that looks happy. So too, it might be hard for children to distinguish angry and disappointed expressions, or surprised and nervous ones. You can avoid this problem by not placing books with such subtle differences side by side. If you choose to include such challenging pairs be prepared to clarify their meanings.

◆ Reread favorite books many times, as children learn a great deal from repeated readings.

### POSSIBILITIES TO EXTEND THE LEARNING

• Ask children to use their own faces and bodies to show a wide range of emotions, moods, or feelings. Be sure to demonstrate yourself.

• Comment on children's emotions and moods during the course of the day.

You look as happy as that Pete the pizza boy.

Are you having a terrible, horrible, no good, very bad day like Alexander?

Of course, you felt scared when the vacuum cleaner made that awful sound, just like the boy was scared when the pretend monster said, "Boo."

• Whenever reading aloud to children, comment on the emotional state of the main characters. Illustrations usually help young children understand the characters' feelings.

• Anne Rogovin, in *Turn Off the TV and Read*, suggests asking children to count to ten using different emotional states. Try counting in a scared way, a surprised way, a happy way, and a sad way, and then ask children to do likewise.

*Look Who's Learning to Read*

# 15. Between the Lines

*ACCOMPLISHMENTS: learning to understand hidden meanings and make inferences*

As children grow as readers, they learn to read between the lines, to understand hidden meanings, and to make inferences. They learn to figure out texts that have gaps in information, and they come to appreciate that sometimes the author says one thing but is actually winking at the reader, hoping the reader will catch on to some inside joke or clever language play.

Successful readers learn that they must bring meaning (all their experiences, all their insights, all their opinions, emotions, concepts, and vocabulary) to the page and build meaning from the page. Reading is not simply calling out words from a text; it is about constructing meaning from the author's ideas as well as your own. In this activity, children are introduced to the experience of filling in gaps by talking about carefully selected songs, poems, and picture books. It is appropriate for most children aged 3 and up.

## MATERIALS TO GATHER

This activity requires carefully selected reading materials. In this case, the traditional verse "A Peanut Sat on the Railroad Track" is used. Many other materials are suggested in Possibilities to Extend the Learning.

## INVITATIONS TO PLAY

◆ Sing the following song several times to children, encouraging them to join in.

> A peanut sat on the railroad track.
> His heart was all a-flutter.
> Around the bend came number 10,
> Toot, toot! Peanut butter!

◆ When you are finished, ask children to explain the song.
  That's a funny song, isn't it? Do you know what it's about?

◆ If children can't explain what happened to the peanut, offer them another way to describe what happened.
  If you were to draw a picture of this song, what would you show?

◆ Don't be discouraged if children can't explain what the song is about. Even though it is a short and seemingly simple verse, there are several concepts children must understand to fully appreciate the meaning of this song:
  • They need to know that peanut butter is made from ground-up peanuts.
  • They need to know that railroad trains can be called by number.
  • They need to know or be able to guess at the meaning of such expressions as "his heart was all a-flutter," and "around the bend."
  • They need to get that a railroad train would crush a peanut that sat on the track.

◆ Explain the meaning of the song to the children, demonstrating how you figured out what was happening.

The person who wrote this song didn't explain exactly what happened to the peanut. Instead, we have to make sense of the words ourselves. We have to picture what was happening.

So a little peanut was sitting on a railroad track—that's where trains roll along. He was afraid he was going to be crushed by a train. No wonder his heart was all a-flutter. Uh-oh, train number ten came around the corner, around the bend. Oh, no he squished the peanut. No wonder the song ends with peanut butter. That's how peanut butter is made, from squished peanuts.

Let's sing it again.

◆ Sing the song again with gusto.

◆ Substitute another food, thereby solidifying children's understanding of the meaning of the song.

Can you think of something else we can sing about? What else could we put on the railroad track and squish it into something good to eat?

◆ Demonstrate a substitution yourself.

What if we sang about a strawberry? If the strawberry got squished, what would it be? Yes, strawberry jam. Let's sing about it.

A strawberry sat on the railroad track.
Her heart was all a-flutter.
Around the bend came number 10.
Toot, toot! Strawberry jam!

◆ Don't worry about not rhyming *flutter* with the last word. Children will delight in changing the food items and will just as eagerly sing without the rhyming last line.

◆ Invite children to suggest other possible substitutions. Try turning a potato into mashed potatoes, an apple into applesauce, or a lemon into lemon juice.

## TIPS TO CONSIDER

◆ Never ask children a barrage of questions about their reading. The point is not to test young children but to joyfully and naturally enrich their understanding. We can help them learn to fill in the blanks by letting them know that writers don't always give us all the information we need; we have to figure things out on our own. We can also help children by demonstrating how we make meaning and by encouraging them to ask questions themselves.

Please ask me questions when you don't understand something I share with you. It's okay to ask, "What does that word mean?" It's okay to ask, "Why did the child do that?" It's okay to ask, "What's happening here?"

## POSSIBILITIES TO EXTEND THE LEARNING

- Be on the lookout for other seemingly simple children's songs, rhymes, and picture books that require reading between the lines. Help children make meaning of them. Help them reach those "aha" moments where they can proudly say, "I get it!"

- Borrow a complete collection of Mother Goose rhymes. Share ones whose meaning is not obvious, including "Three Wise Men of Gotham," "Little Polly Flinders," "Jack Sprat," and even the riddle poem "Humpty Dumpty."

- Borrow Kristine O'Connell George's poetry collection *Little Dog Poems*. These beautifully crafted short poems demand that readers fill in the blanks to fully understand how the little dog spends his day. Encourage children to pay attention to the illustrations, as they will help youngsters make meaning.

- Share a book of jokes for very young children. Help children understand the punch lines, asking, "Do you get it?"

- Share *Never Give a Fish an Umbrella and Other Silly Presents* by Mike Thaler. Probe children's understanding of the humorous statements.

- Share picture books with very surprising endings, ones that demand that the children "read" the final illustrations. These include *Just Like Everyone Else* by Karla Kuskin, Jan Peck's *Way Down Deep in the Deep Blue Sea*, *Way Far Away on a Wild Safari*, and *Way Up High in a Tall Green Tree*, Peggy Rathmann's *Good Night, Gorilla*, Andrew Clements's *Workshop*, and "Peter Perfect," a chapter in Bernard Waber's book *Nobody Is Perfick*.

- Share picture books whose last lines demand rereading and pausing to see if children get the meaning. These include Barbara Bottner's *Be Brown*, Shirley Neitzel's rebus story, *I'm Taking a Trip on My Train*, Simon James's *Leon and Bob*, and Karma Wilson's *A Frog in the Bog*. Peter Sis's *Going Up: A Color Counting Book* also provides young children with the experience of building meaning and offers a joyful, surprising ending.

# 16. Questions Galore

*ACCOMPLISHMENTS: learning to question the world and texts*

As soon as most young children learn the word *why*, they seem to never stop asking that question. And that is a very good thing. Children need to keep on asking questions, those beginning with *why* as well as those beginning with *where*, *which*, *when*, *do*, *can*, and *how*. And of course, they need a grown-up to take their questions seriously and to attempt to answer them, no matter how challenging and time-consuming that may be. As children grow older and enter school, they need to be encouraged to continue asking questions, not merely answering them. Not only will they learn new vocabulary, concepts, and information, but they will become better readers when they ask questions of the books they are reading. In this activity, children learn the importance of asking questions by listening to carefully selected picture books, ones that demonstrate the power of asking questions. This activity is appropriate for all children who have begun to ask "Why?"

## MATERIALS TO GATHER

Here, the picture book *Why Do Kittens Purr?* by Marion Dane Bauer is shared. Other appropriate titles are listed in Possibilities to Extend the Learning.

## INVITATIONS TO PLAY

◆ Talk to children about the importance of asking questions.

   I love when you ask me questions. Your questions show me that you are thinking and learning and growing. Lately, you have been asking me lots of questions that begin with *why*. I just love those questions. Even grown-ups learn by asking questions. Sometimes we ask "Why" questions, but sometimes we ask other kinds of questions.

◆ Make use of your setting to demonstrate real questions.

   Let's play a game, right here in this elevator. I'll share three questions I have about elevators and then it will be your turn to ask three questions.

   I'd like to know, "What makes the elevator go up and down?"

   And the sign right here says that only ten people are allowed on the elevator at a time. I'd like to know, "How come only ten people are allowed?"

   And here it says that the elevator gets inspected, gets checked out. I want to know, "Why does it have to be inspected, and what does the inspector look for?"

◆ Demonstrate how you might get answers for your questions.

   I might have to read a book about elevators to find out how they work. And maybe I can talk to the elevator inspector the next time she comes to find out about the number of people allowed and what she checks out on the elevator.

◆ Invite children to ask questions.

Is there anything that you'd like to know about elevators?

◆ Celebrate the questions the children ask. If they ask, "When will I be tall enough to reach the highest buttons?" "How come there aren't any windows in this elevator?" and "Why is there an L button and a B button?" you might reply:

Those are great questions. You asked "When?" and "How come?" and "Why?"

◆ Suggest ways to get questions answered.

I can answer your last question. Those letters stand for special floors in this apartment building. The L stands for Lobby, the floor we come in on, and the B stands for Basement, the underground floor where the washers and dryers are.

I think we need to ask your doctor when you might be tall enough to reach the highest button. Let's see how many inches your arm has to grow for you to reach the top button. It looks like you need another three inches. The next time you get a checkup we can ask your pediatrician how long it might take for a child's arm to grow three inches.

And I think we can ask the custodian about why there are no windows in this elevator. He can probably explain that best because he knows a lot about how buildings are constructed.

◆ Remind children to always speak up when they have questions.

Wherever we go, whatever we are doing, you should ask the questions you have. That way you will learn so many new things.

◆ Throughout the day, continue modeling your own questions and encouraging children to ask theirs. Play the three-question game when you are riding on the bus, looking at dogs in the street, or spotting appropriate photographs in the newspaper.

◆ Read and discuss Marion Dane Bauer's *Why Do Kittens Purr?* Point out how much the boy is learning by asking questions. Be sure to clarify the answers provided if the children need more information.

## TIPS TO CONSIDER

◆ Children can ask very challenging questions, including those that may be too difficult to respond to when children are very young. It's okay to tell children, "I don't know, but we can find out!" or "It will be easier to explain that to you when you are older."

◆ Young children can ask a flood of "Why?" questions, one right after the other. It sometimes takes a lot of patience to answer them. At some point you may have to suggest, "I don't have time to answer that question, but I will write it down so I can answer it later." Be sure to write it down and return to it.

◆ Remind children that asking questions shows how clever, curious, and eager they are to learn.

## POSSIBILITIES TO EXTEND THE LEARNING

- Borrow nonfiction picture books to extend the information about animals contained in *Why Do Kittens Purr?*

- Share additional picture books that encourage children to ask questions. These include the following:
  *Do Kangaroos Wear Seatbelts?* by Jane Kurtz
  *"Hi, Pizza Man!"* by Virginia Walter
  *It's Bedtime, Wibbly Pig!* by Mick Inkpen
  *Owly* by Mike Thaler
  *When Winter Comes* by Nancy Van Laan
  *Where, Where Is Swamp Bear?* by Kathi Appelt
  *Why Is the Sky Blue?* by Sally Grindley
  *Would You Rather . . .* by John Burningham

# RHYMING WORDS

## 17. Fabric Rhymes

*ACCOMPLISHMENTS: expanding vocabulary and concepts, rhyming words*

This activity taps into young children's interest in touching everything within their reach. Children will learn the names of various common fabrics, expand their vocabulary, and have an opportunity to rhyme words. This activity is appropriate for children aged 3 and up.

## MATERIALS TO GATHER

Gather a pile of garments made of different fabrics or small swatches of material from your sewing supplies. If you use flannel, silk, cotton, wool, satin, lace, corduroy, denim, leather, and suede, you can share the simple rhymes printed below. If you choose other fabrics, be prepared to create your own rhymes.

## INVITATIONS TO PLAY

◆ Introduce the activity.

See that pile of clothing over there? Some of those things are yours, but most are mine.

We are not going to play dress-up, and we are not going to do the laundry or visit the cleaners.

Instead, we are going to play a game with these garments (articles of clothing).

First, I am going to teach you what each of these materials is called.

Each one of them is made of a different fabric. Rub your fingers over them—don't they feel different?

Which ones feel soft?

Which ones feel rough?

Do any feel itchy?

Do any feel smooth?

This one is made of _____.

This one is made of _____.

This fabric is called _____.

This fabric is called _____.

◆ Continue until all fabrics are named. To reinforce the names and help children feel comfortable using these new words, you might ask children such questions as:

What material would be good for your pillowcase?

What material would be good for a tablecloth?

What material would be good for your jeans?

What material would be good for a bride?

What material would be good for your blanket?

What material would be good for a winter jacket?

What material would be good for a swimsuit?

You might also hold up items and ask such questions as these:

Do you remember what my blue shirt is made of?

Do you remember what my fancy hat is made of?

Do you remember what your overalls are made of?

Do you remember what Grandpa's scarf is made of?

◆ When children recall the names of most of the fabrics, you can share the rhymes listed below, omitting the last word (the fabric name). Ask children to complete the rhyme and select the corresponding fabric.

Change the channel. Dress in _____ (flannel).

Drink your milk. Dress in _____ (silk).

Eggs are rotten. Dress in _____ (cotton).

Push and pull. Dress in _____ (wool).

Dance to Latin. Dress in _____ (satin).

Fly to space. Dress in _____ (lace).

Jump for joy. Dress in _____ (corduroy).

Snakes have venom. Dress in _____ (denim).

Tickle with a feather. Dress in _____ (leather).

Watch a parade. Dress in _____ (suede).

## TIPS TO CONSIDER

◆ If you choose different fabrics and create your own rhymes, avoid fabric names that are difficult to rhyme (e.g., acrylic).

◆ Be sure to stress the sound of the rhyming word in the first line to make it easier for children to fill in the rhyming fabric name.

◆ Limit the activity to only three or four fabrics at a time if children seem overwhelmed by too many new words.

## POSSIBILITIES TO EXTEND THE LEARNING

- Encourage children to note other fabrics in their homes, always asking for their precise names. If possible, invent rhymes to add to the list.

- Take a tour of a department store, clothing store, or sewing shop, touching the materials and discussing the names of fabrics.

- If children are old enough to memorize the first lines, reverse roles: children announce the first line, and you supply the rhyming second.

- Use the complete chant as a jump-rope rhyme.

- Create rhymes around the names of designs on children's clothing. Below are a few possibilities:
  Don't be sad. Wear some _____ (plaid).
  If it's hot, wear _____ (polka dot).
  Out of wipes? Wear some _____ (stripes).
  It's not a rag. It's _____ (zigzag).

- A similar activity can be created using building materials (glass, steel, brick, plastic, wood, ceramic, concrete, etc.) that are found in the home and neighborhood. Point out materials and then create rhymes to fill in. Below are a few possibilities.
  It's fantastic. You chose _____ (plastic).
  It's no trick. You chose _____ (brick).
  It's a treat. You chose _____ (concrete).
  If you could, you'd choose _____ (wood).
  It's for real. You chose _____ (steel).
  Think I'll pass, if you choose _____ (glass).
  Can't build a hammock, if you choose _____ (ceramic).

# 18. Swing Rhymes

*ACCOMPLISHMENTS: expanding vocabulary, rhyming words*

This outdoor activity enriches the playground experience by combining gleeful swinging with the chanting of a rhyming verse. Young children will learn new vocabulary and receive practice in listening to and calling out rhyming words. Appropriate for all ages of children who can be placed in a swing.

## MATERIALS TO GATHER

This activity requires no gathering of materials. You simply need to learn the simple rhymes listed below or create your own.

## INVITATIONS TO PLAY

◆ As you push children, begin chanting any or all of the following rhymes.

◆ Add excitement by attempting to touch the body part mentioned as the children swing forward. There is no need to actually complete the gesture. Children love the sense of adventure in possibly being caught.

Swing high
Swing low,
Now I'll touch your little toe.

Swing to the sky,
Swing to the trees.
Now I'll touch your little knees.

Swing to the north,
Swing to the south.
Now I'll touch your little mouth.

Swing in the breeze,
Swing in the air.
Now I'll touch your dark brown hair.

Swing rough,
Swing calm.
Now I'll touch your little palm.

(You may have to point to your own palm to clarify for children. Of course, if children are holding on safely, you will never be able to touch their palm.)

Swing to the east
Swing to the west,
Now I'll touch your little chest.

Swing to the birds,
Swing to the leaves.
Now I'll touch your little sleeves.

Swing out,
Swing in.
Now I'll touch your little chin.

Swing up,
Swing down.
Now I'll touch your little crown.
(You may have to explain that crown refers to head.)

Swing left,
Swing right.
Now I'll try to take a bite!
(Of course, just pretend.)

## TIPS TO CONSIDER

◆ Safety first. Make sure children do not attempt to let go in order to touch their own body parts.

◆ If children do not know the names of the body parts, they will learn them as you chant, point them out, and pretend to touch them.

◆ You might want to learn one verse for each playground visit, until children are familiar with all the body parts.

## POSSIBILITIES TO EXTEND THE LEARNING

- You can share each verse, leaving off the last word and inviting children to fill in the rhyming body part.

- You can chant any nursery rhyme or sing any favorite song as you push children on a swing. It is a prime time for children to hear rhymes and a perfect way to eliminate what can become a monotonous act for adult caregivers.

- Rather than offering rhymes, try saying good-bye in different ways each time you push children away. You might include the following:

  Adios

  Au revoir

  Arrivederci

  Shalom

  Hasta mañana

  Hasta luego

  Good-bye

  So long

  See you later, alligator

  In a little while, crocodile

  Sayonara

  Bon voyage

  Farewell

# 19. Bath-Time Rhymes

*ACCOMPLISHMENTS: expanding vocabulary and concepts, rhyming words*

This activity fills bath time with laughter and learning, enriching the experience for children. It combines getting to know names on a world map with practice in rhyming names of parts of the body. Children of all ages can listen to the rhyme and learn the names of body parts. Children aged 3½ and up will appreciate the map viewing.

## MATERIALS TO GATHER

It would be very helpful to have a world map or a globe. (Books containing maps can be borrowed from school or public libraries.) Other than learning the rhymes listed below, no preparation is needed.

## INVITATIONS TO PLAY

◆ Begin with map exploration.

> Today I want to show you where we live on this big map.
>
> Our country has a name, just like every child has a name.
>
> Our country is called the United States of America, and it is right here.

(Your city and/or state can also be pointed out, and if any family members or friends live far away or come from foreign lands, be sure and point out those places as well.)

> The people in different countries speak different languages, live in different kinds of homes, wear different kinds of clothes, eat different kinds of foods, and even wash up in different ways. But we are all human beings who need to take care of one another.
>
> Now I am going to point out some really faraway places.
>
> These three islands are in the Mediterranean Sea: Sicily, Rhodes, and Crete.

◆ Ask children to pronounce the names after you say them.

◆ Do not expect the children to remember the names; just encourage them to delight in the sounds of the words.

> Now I am going to show you three countries that are in South America. Here is Ecuador, here is Peru, and here is Uruguay.
>
> Some countries are made up of states, like our country. Now I am going to show you three states in the southern part of our country. Here is Georgia, here is Alabama, and here is Tennessee.
>
> States are filled with lots of cities. We live in New York City. (Mention a few others that the children may have heard of.) But we have friends who live in other cities like Newark and Boston and Stamford.
>
> Now I am going to show you a few cities on the map.
>
> This is the city called Prague. It's in a country called the Czech Republic.
>
> This is the city called Vienna. It's in a country called Austria.
>
> This is the city called Budapest. It's in a country called Hungary.
>
> This country is called Canada, and I am going to show you where three Canadian cities are.

This is Toronto, this is Montreal, and this is Winnipeg.

Now I'm going to show you three cities in Colorado, another state in the United States. This is Denver, this is Aspen, and this is Boulder.

◆ Remember to encourage children to say the names aloud.

There are a few more countries I want to show you. These three are near one another: This one is called Norway, this one is called Denmark, and this one is called Sweden.

And these are three more countries that are near one another. This one is called England, this one is called France, and this one is called Spain.

◆ Children may be interested to hear the languages spoken in these countries. You could point out that people in England speak English, people in France speak French, and people in Spain speak Spanish.

I have a few rhymes that mention all these places, but I am going to wait until bath time to share them with you. Should we fill up the tub right now?

◆ Share rhyming verses with children as they play in the bathtub. You might want to chant each of them a few times, adding your own rhythmic beat. Be sure to stress the final rhyming words in each line.

Sicily, Rhodes, Crete,
Now it's time to wash your feet.

Denver, Aspen, Boulder,
Now it's time to wash your shoulder.

Ecuador, Peru, Uruguay,
Now it's time to wash your thigh.

Georgia Alabama, Tennessee
Now it's time to wash your knee.

Prague, Vienna, Budapest,
Now it's time to wash your chest.

Toronto, Montreal, Winnipeg,
Now it's time to wash your leg.

◆ Expect laughter after the next verse as well as after the final verse.

Norway, Denmark, Sweden,
Now it's time to wash your feet again!

England, France, Spain,
Now it's time to wash your brain!
What? Wash your brain?

This time I am going to say the rhyme, but I am going to leave off the last word and you can guess the missing word.

Sicily, Rhodes, Crete,
Now it's time to wash your _____.

Denver, Aspen, Boulder,
Now it's time to wash your _____.

◆ Continue leaving off the final word in all the verses, encouraging the children to guess the missing, rhyming body part.

## TIPS TO CONSIDER

◆ Take time to learn the rhymes yourself. Begin with just one and share additional ones as you learn them.

◆ Change the order of the verses, making them match your method of bathing children. (You may not want to begin with feet washing.)

◆ There's no need to use the map if children seem too immature. You can simply tell them that you are going to share the names of different faraway places from all over the world.

◆ Ask your librarian for a copy or recording of *My Aunt Came Back*, a traditional folk song that incorporates faraway lands and contains engaging rhymes. Share with children.

◆ Encourage children to use these exotic settings in their dramatic play. For example, you may say:
   Are you a pilot flying a plane? Where are you headed? To Crete?
   Oh, no, your doll is moving? No wonder you look so sad. Where is she going? To England? Well, you can write to her or call her on the telephone. The people speak English in England.
   Are you having a tea party? Where are your guests coming from? Will anyone be visiting from Sweden or Norway?

## POSSIBILITIES TO EXTEND THE LEARNING

• Share verses upon leaving the bath, substituting the word *dry* for *wash*.

• Make up additional verses, using other locales and body parts.

• Show the words on paper to older preschoolers or early childhood siblings, pointing out how different letters can make the same sound (for example, the *uay* in *Uruguay* and the *igh* in *thigh*; the *ete* in *Crete* and the *eet* in *feet*).

• Encourage children's curiosity about different places, answering their questions and researching the answers if necessary.

# 20. Mealtime Rhymes

*ACCOMPLISHMENTS: rhyming words, learning new vocabulary, forming questions*

Mealtime is the perfect opportunity for conversation as well as language play. After repeated presentations, children will be able to fill in the missing word when you chant the beginning of the mealtime rhymes below. As children develop an ear for rhyme, they will use new vocabulary and invent their own rhyming food questions. This activity is appropriate for children aged 2½ and up.

## MATERIALS TO GATHER

This activity requires very little preparation other than learning a few rhymes or inventing your own. In the second rhyming game, the rhymes will depend on the food being served.

## INVITATIONS TO PLAY

◆ When children are attempting to feed themselves, encourage them with a chant about filling the spoon. Each time the children scoop up their yogurt, macaroni and cheese, or applesauce, you can share the following chants.

> Fill your spoon,
> Mama comes soon.

> Fill your spoon,
> Act like a baboon.

> Fill your spoon,
> Pop a balloon.

> Fill your spoon,
> Fly to the moon.

> Fill your spoon,
> Sing a great tune.

> Fill your spoon,
> See the caterpillar's cocoon.

> Fill your spoon,
> Watch out for the typhoon.

> Fill your spoon,
> Paint the wall maroon.

◆ When children have finished eating, repeat each verse, omitting the last word.

This time, I am going to say the same rhymes again, but I am going to leave off the last word. See if you can fill in the word that rhymes and makes sense.

Fill your spoon
Mama comes _____ (soon).

Fill your spoon
Act like a _____ (baboon).

Continue repeating other verses, completing them if children cannot.

◆ During mealtime, when several foods are spread across the table, create appropriate rhymes to share.

It doesn't tickle.
Eat a pickle.

I'm not pickin'.
Eat some chicken.

Don't be a phony.
Eat some macaroni.

Won't you please
Eat some cheese?

Blow a horn.
Eat some corn.

A tooth is loose.
Drink some juice.

You're amazin'.
Eat a raisin.

Stop that huffin'.
Eat your muffin.

◆ Again, after the meal you can repeat the rhymes, omitting the last word and asking the children to supply it.
Now I am going to repeat the rhymes, but I am going to leave off the last word. See if you can fill in the word that rhymes and makes sense.

It doesn't tickle.
Eat a _____ (pickle).

I'm not pickin'.
Eat some _____ (chicken).

Continue with additional verses, completing them if children cannot.

◆ For older children, introduce a question game that calls for animal names that rhyme with food names.

> I have an idea. I am going to ask you a rhyming question about animals and what they might eat.

◆ Begin with simple, one-syllable rhyming animal and food names.

> Would a snake eat a cake?
>
> Would a bear eat a pear?
>
> Would mice eat rice?

◆ Invite children to join in the fun, creating their own animal-food rhyming questions. Some additional examples follow:

> Would a fish eat a knish?
>
> Would a pig eat a fig?

◆ If children understand the challenge, introduce two-syllable animal-food rhyming questions.

> Would a parrot eat a carrot?
>
> Would a turkey eat some jerky?
>
> Would a raccoon eat a stewed prune?
>
> Would a poodle eat a noodle?
>
> Would a puffin eat a muffin?

◆ You can then proceed to even lengthier animal-food rhyming questions.

> Would an elephant eat a peppermint?
>
> Would a butterfly eat an apple pie?
>
> Would an antelope eat a cantaloupe?
>
> Would a chimpanzee eat some fricassee?
>
> Would a kangaroo eat some beef stew?
>
> Would a wildebeest eat a holiday feast?

## TIPS TO CONSIDER

◆ Don't hesitate to use such "million-dollar" words as *cocoon*, *typhoon*, and *maroon*. Be sure to explain their meaning to children, though.

◆ Explain any unfamiliar animals you introduce, as well as any new foods. Some appear in the rhyming questions below.

> Would a gnu eat stew?
>
> Would a mule eat gruel?
>
> Would a giraffe eat rice pilaf?
>
> Would a quetzal eat a pretzel?
>
> Would a billy goat eat an ice cream float?
>
> Would a big fat toad eat pie à la mode?

◆ Accept words that are not perfect rhymes.

> Would a mallard eat a salad?
>
> Would a goldfish eat a sandwich?
>
> Would a horse eat sauce?

◆ Young children's mispronunciations as well as regional dialect differences create rhyming challenges.

## POSSIBILITIES TO EXTEND THE LEARNING

- Try and research answers to questions such as whether an antelope would eat a cantaloupe or a chimpanzee would eat fricassee.

- Create additional food rhymes as well as animal-food rhyming questions.

- Ask your public librarian for collections of children's food poems. Borrow a few anthologies and find a few favorites. Share with children around mealtime. A few titles follow:

  *Hot Potato: Mealtime Rhymes* by Neil Philip

  *I Scream, You Scream: A Feast of Food Rhymes* by Lillian Morrison

  *Tea Party Today: Poems to Sip and Savor* by Eileen Spinelli

  *Yummy! Eating Through a Day* by Lee Bennett Hopkins (ed.)

- Use other occasions to create fun rhyming activities. For example, while walking down the street, encourage children to step over the cracks in the pavement with such rhymes as:

  Step on a crack,
  Lose your backpack.

  Step on a crack,
  Drop your snack.

  Step on a crack,
  Scratch my back.

# 21. Color Rhyme Questions

*ACCOMPLISHMENTS: learning new vocabulary, rhyming words, forming questions*

This activity invites youngsters to play with language. The questions that follow challenge children to think about the colors of common objects as well as the sounds of rhyming words. In addition to reviewing the names of ordinary colors, children will learn the names of more unusual ones as well as the names of new objects. Older children can be asked to create their own rhyming questions. This activity is appropriate for children aged 2½ and up.

## MATERIALS TO GATHER

Other than thinking about rhyming the names of colors with objects, as in the sample questions listed below, this activity requires no special preparation. A small box of crayons can be used to review colors before beginning to play.

## INVITATIONS TO PLAY

◆ Introduce the activity.

> I am going to ask you some funny questions today. Each time I pull a crayon out of the box, I am going to ask you a question about that color. And you can answer yes or no. Are you ready?

◆ Pulling out the red crayon, you might ask:

> Have you ever seen a red bed? A red sled? A redhead? A red shed?

◆ Explain the meaning of words such as *shed* or *sled* if they are new for children.

◆ Encourage children to ask about the meaning of any unfamiliar words.

◆ Provide lots of examples to clarify the meaning, showing items or drawing pictures if necessary.

◆ Engage children in conversations about any new concepts.

> Where have you seen a red bed?
>
> Do we know any redheads?
>
> What do you think people keep in their sheds?
>
> When do you think a sled would come in handy?

◆ Continue in a similar manner with other colors, always taking the opportunity to extend children's responses. See comments in parentheses.

> Have you ever seen a blue shoe? (Who wears blue shoes?)
>
> A blue zoo? (Zoos usually have so many colors.)
>
> A blue gnu? (There's a picture of a gnu in the dictionary. It looks like a buffalo.)
>
> Blue poo? (Yes, that is a very silly question.)

Have you ever seen a black snack? (Have you ever tasted black jelly beans or licorice?)

A black tack? (Thumbtacks are usually silver. Pushpins come in many colors.)

A black sack? (I think we have a sack of potatoes in the kitchen, but I don't think the sack is black.)

A black backpack? (That's right. My backpack is black.)

Have you ever seen a white knight? (I think there is a picture of a knight in shining armor in our fairy-tale book.)

A white light? (Are all of our electric bulbs white in color?)

A white kite? (Was our kite solid white, or did it have designs on it?)

A green bean? (My favorite green beans are string beans.)

A yellow cello? (Do you think a cello sounds like a violin?)

Yellow Jell-O? (What flavor would yellow Jell-O be?)

A pink sink? (I think Aunt Alison has a pink sink.)

A pink mink? (This furry little animal is usually dark brown, but maybe its nose is pink.)

A brown crown? (I think most kings and queens wear gold crowns.)

A tan fan? (People use electric fans to cool themselves off. I can fold a paper fan for you.)

A gray day? (Gray days are cloudy and overcast.)

◆ With older children, include more challenging rhyming questions such as the following:

Have you ever seen turquoise toys? (Let's see if we have any toys that are turquoise in color.)

A teal seal? (Yes, teal is a greenish blue. Do you like it?)

Gold mold? (Mold grows on very old food. Have you ever seen mold? It's often green in color.)

A chartreuse moose? (I've only seen brown moose and black moose. Chartreuse is a yellowish green.)

A maroon baboon? (I've only seen black and brown baboons. Maroon is a dark red. I have a maroon sweater.)

## TIPS TO CONSIDER

◆ Avoid *orange*, *silver*, and *purple* in rhyming activities. Let older children know why these color words are not used.

Can you think of anything that rhymes with *orange*, *purple*, or *silver*?

◆ When using unusual colors such as turquoise, teal, chartreuse, and maroon, it would be helpful to have an example of that color to point out. In other words, have that maroon sweater handy.

## POSSIBILITIES TO EXTEND THE LEARNING

- Invite children to create their own rhyming questions. You and your children can take turns asking questions. Be accepting of very silly suggestions or words that don't really rhyme. For example, "Have you ever seen a violet pilot?"

- Point out the names of colors printed on most crayon wrappers. Attempt to create rhyming questions with these.

- Encourage children to name the colors of cars in the street, items in the laundry basket, or socks in their drawer. Use these colors for rhyming questions.

- Ask for paint charts in your hardware store. Share with children, reading the names of the colors. Make up rhyming questions if possible.

# 22. Silly Statement Puppet Play

*ACCOMPLISHMENTS: rhyming words, paying attention to verbs, engaging in dramatic play*

This activity capitalizes on children's interest in playing with puppets as well as their interest in silly situations and conversations. The activity provides abundant opportunities for children to listen for rhymes and pay attention to verbs (action words). It is appropriate for children aged 2½ and up, with older children taking a more active role in the puppet conversations.

## MATERIALS TO GATHER

This activity requires two hand or finger puppets. Homemade sock or paper-bag puppets will work just as well as store-bought ones. Grown-ups can refer to the lines listed below or create original ones. The following samples can serve as models.

## INVITATIONS TO PLAY

◆ Place a puppet on each hand and turn them toward each other so they appear to be talking.

> Today I am going to put on a puppet show for you.
>
> These two puppets are going to talk to each other.

◆ Introduce the two puppets, announcing names for each.

> This one is very chatty and always talks first.
>
> This other one likes to tease her friend and sometimes can be very silly.
>
> Are you ready to be a great listener?

You can keep a copy of these short lines near you to use as a script.

| | |
|---|---|
| Puppet #1: | I like to go to the park. |
| Puppet #2: | Well, I like to go to the shark! |
| Puppet #1: | Oh, no! That's very dangerous! |
| | |
| Puppet #1: | I like to sleep in my bed. |
| Puppet #2: | Well, I like to sleep in my sled. |
| Puppet #1: | Oh, that doesn't sound comfortable! |
| | |
| Puppet #1: | I like to eat figs. |
| Puppet #2: | Well, I like to eat twigs! |
| Puppet #1: | What? Are you an elephant? |

◆ Continue sharing more short conversations as long as children are engaged. Additional possibilities follow.

> I like blue balloons.
>
> Well, I like blue baboons!
>
> What? I've never seen a blue baboon!

I like to skip in my school.

Well, I like to skip in my pool.

No, that's silly! You can't skip in water!

I like to jump with a rope.

Well, I like to jump with soap.

What? That's ridiculous and that would be slippery. Never jump with soap!

I can eat a hot dog.

Well I can eat a warthog.

A warthog? I've never heard of anyone eating a warthog!

I can brush my hair.

I can brush my chair.

Why would you do that? Is it dusty or covered with lint?

I like to play with clay.

Well, I like to play with hay.

What? Are you a pony?

I like to polish my nails.

Well, I like to polish my tails.

What? You don't have a tail and you certainly don't have two tails.

I like to drink juice.

Well, I like to drink a moose.

What? You can't drink a moose. That's absurd.

I like to climb a tree.

Well, I like to climb a bee.

That's impossible. You can't climb a bee. They're so small and they sting if you bother them.

I like to plant flowers.

Well, I like to plant towers.

Silly you. You have to build towers, not plant them. (Do you remember that tall block tower we once built?)

I like to eat at the table.

Well, I like to eat in a stable.

Maybe you really are a pony!

I like to ride in a car.

Well, I like to ride on a star.

Are you an astronaut?

I like to wear a hat.

Well, I like to wear a bat.

Do you mean a baseball bat or a bat that hangs upside down in trees at night? You know, it doesn't really matter which one you choose because you can't wear either one on your head.

On my birthday cake, I like to put candles.

Well, on my birthday cake, I like to put sandals.

Yuck! That's ridiculous. You can't put shoes on your food!

I want a pet puppy

Well, I want a pet guppy.

Okay. Now that makes sense!

◆ If children seem ready, invite them to take the role of puppet #2. Remind them to listen carefully so they will be able to repeat the phrase, substituting an appropriate rhyming ending.

## TIPS TO CONSIDER

◆ When making the first statement, state the verb clearly and stress the end word to make it easier for older children to create a rhyming answer.

◆ When responding to children's rhyming statements, don't hesitate to use such sophisticated words as *shocking*, *absurd*, or *ridiculous*, as children catch on quickly to words used in meaningful ways.

◆ Children will likely attempt to recall the responses that you have already shared. Celebrate their ability to remember these.

◆ If children create nonsense words, accept them, congratulating them for attempting to rhyme.

◆ Explain any new concepts. For example, show a photo of a guppy if children are unfamiliar with this animal.

## POSSIBILITIES TO EXTEND LEARNING

• Save the puppet conversations in written form for when children are older and can read dialogue on their own.

• Use puppets to continue conversations in dramatic play. In other words, encourage children to invent stories about a child who sleeps in a sled, plays with hay, or rides on a star.

• Help children create their own rhyming puppet conversations.

# ALPHABET STUDY/
# SOUND-SYMBOL CORRESPONDENCE

## 23. Alphabet Play

*ACCOMPLISHMENTS: recognizing letters of the alphabet, learning names of letters*

The activities below are intended to help children recognize the letters of the alphabet and become familiar with their names, all in joyful and natural ways. Many young children learn to sing the alphabet song ("Now I Know My ABCs") before they are able to identify letters of the alphabet. (Those children are often surprised to discover that *l-m-n-o-p* represents five separate letters.) Then too, many children learn to recognize letters and call out their names (letter identification) without associating those letters with the sounds they represent (phonemic awareness). Some children do learn letter names and sounds simultaneously, particularly those who learn the alphabet through alphabet books, becoming familiar with such phrases as "B is for ___." Learning to write the letters occurs much later for most children. The letter name activities described below are intended for all children who express an interest in learning the alphabet.

## MATERIALS TO GATHER

You can use any alphabet chart with a clear representation of the 26 letters. A homemade one will do, as will a poster, place mat, or page from a picture book. Uppercase letters (capitals) are enough for now.

You will also need additional uppercase letters that can be manipulated. Foam letters for the bath work well, as do alphabet cookie cutters, alphabet puzzle pieces, alphabet stencils, alphabet stamp pads, alphabet blocks, alphabet decals, alphabet stickers, alphabet ice cube molds, alphabet magnets, and alphabet-shaped pasta or cereal.

## INVITATIONS TO PLAY

◆ To do this activity, children must be familiar with the alphabet song. Sing the song frequently with children, inviting them to join in as soon as they are able.

A, B, C, D / E, F, G / H, I, J, K / L, M, N, O, P / Q, R, S / T, U, V / W, X, Y, and Z. / Now I know my ABCs. / Next time won't you sing with me?

◆ Display an alphabet chart.

Today when we sing the alphabet song, I am going to point to each letter as we sing.

◆ Sing slowly enough to be able to point to each letter as you sing its name.

◆ If children seem ready and interested, invite them to sing on their own.

This time, why don't you sing the song by yourself and I'll point to each letter?

◆ If children seem ready and interested, invite them to do the pointing.

This time, why don't I sing the song and you do the pointing?

◆ If children continue to be interested in learning the names of the letters, you might continue your play by introducing an alphabet sequencing activity. Use any of the alphabet manipulatives listed above.

Do you see this box (basket, bag, envelope) filled with letters? Let's try to put them in order, beginning with A-B-C. As we work, we'll sing the song to help us remember the order of the letters.

## TIPS TO CONSIDER

◆ Many alphabet charts present uppercase and lowercase letters together. Don't expect children to recall all of them at once. Lowercase *b*, *d*, *p*, and *q* are particularly difficult for young children to distinguish at first. Follow children's leads, answering any questions they ask about lowercase letters.

◆ Many alphabet charts contain illustrations to support children's learning of the sounds connected to each letter. Make sure that children know the names of the objects presented. In other words, if there are mittens next to the letter *M* make sure that the children are not calling them gloves.

## POSSIBILITIES TO EXTEND THE LEARNING

• Point out letters in your everyday environment. For example, the *H* and *C* on faucet handles, the *G*, *L*, and *B*, on elevator buttons, the letters on apartment doors (e.g., 2C), and even the F. B. I. copyright message on DVDs.

• Select an advertisement from a newspaper that has many uppercase letters. Give children highlighter pens, asking them to mark the letters they know, or help them find all the letters of the alphabet.

• Use alphabet blocks to create signs for the home. For example, spell out *WELCOME* and place the letters on a shelf near the front door. Spell out *BOOKS* and place atop a bookcase. Ask children to help you make the signs by handing you needed letters.

Can you give me a *W*?

Now I need an *E*.

Next comes *L* . . .

• Pretend-write letters of the alphabet on children's backs, asking them to guess the letter you are tracing.

• Search for letter formations made from surprising objects in the home. For example, the ladder from a toy fire truck looks like a *Z* when folded, opened scissors can look like an *X*, and a chair can look like a lowercase *h*.

- Borrow or buy Stephen T. Johnson's book *Alphabet City*. Share with children, asking them to trace the letters with their fingers. Then take a neighborhood walk, looking for letter formations made from surprising objects in your community.

- Using a jump rope, form as many letters as possible on the ground, asking children to identify them. When they are ready, invite children to use the jump rope to form letters themselves. Some letters will be easier than others. You might want to begin with *I, J, M, N, O, S, U, V, W,* and *Z.*

- Older children, 4- and 5-year-olds, might begin forming letters on the sidewalk with chalk or using a paintbrush and water on a chalkboard.

- Take a neighborhood walk, reading the letters on the license plates of parked cars. Make the game more challenging by attempting to find all 26 on one outing. (You'll probably need to carry a handwritten copy of the alphabet and a crayon, crossing off the letters as the children spot them. Otherwise, it will be difficult to recall which ones you've already seen and not seen. Children may enjoy holding the copy as you stroll the neighborhood.)

- Using a dark marker, write the 26 uppercase letters in large, clear block letters. Ask children to search for shapes in the letters. Provide crayons for children to color in the shapes.
    Which letters have circles in them? (*C, O, Q*)
    Which have triangles? (*A, K, M, N, R, V, W, X, Y, Z*)
    Which have semicircles? (*B, D, P, R*)
    Do any have rectangles? (*E, F, H, L, T*)
    Depending on your handwriting, some letters may suggest squares rather than rectangles and ovals rather than circles. Point out that some shapes are not complete, but if you color in the area, the shapes will be easier to see. For example, you can create a rectangle from an *L* by adding two other sides. You can create two rectangles from the letter *T*. If children don't know all the shapes, take this opportunity to teach them.

- Place a toy letter (magnet, puzzle piece, or foam letter) in a paper bag. Ask children to guess the letter just from feeling the shape. Continue concealing letters and asking children to guess.

- Using toy letters, play the What's Missing? game. Select five letters randomly, not those in any alphabetical sequence. Have children name each and then cover their eyes. Remove one letter, asking children, "Which one is missing?" Let children take turns hiding letters and asking you to guess. Continue playing by selecting five different letters.

- When children seem ready and interested, call their attention to lowercase letters. You may want to start with those in the child's name. Eventually, you can have them match uppercase letters with lowercase ones.

# 24. A Is for Apple

*ACCOMPLISHMENTS: reading alphabet books, learning sound-symbol correspondence, expanding vocabulary and concepts*

This activity involves the reading aloud of alphabet books, a major way in which children begin to connect letter names with the sounds associated with them. Well-designed alphabet books also introduce new vocabulary and concepts to young children and spark interesting conversations. This activity is appropriate for children aged 2½ and up.

## MATERIALS TO GATHER

Here, the book being used is *ABC Pop!* by Rachel Isadora, an alphabet book that should be readily available in the children's section of most public libraries. Any interesting alphabet book can work just as well.

## INVITATIONS TO PLAY

◆ Introduce the book.

I borrowed another alphabet book from the library today. It's called *ABC Pop!* It was written by a woman named Rachel Isadora. I think we have read many other books she has written. She also did the illustrations for her alphabet book. She must have worked very hard to make the pictures and the words.

Would you like to sing the alphabet song before we read this alphabet book?

◆ Share each page, chatting about the pictures as well as the letters of the alphabet.

Yes, *A* is for *airplane*.

Look here, the author even included the sounds that airplanes make. She wrote "zoom" and "voom" and "biz biz." Do you hear any noises when we see airplanes flying in the sky?

Yes, *B* is for *buildings*.

That building looks like the Empire State Building, a very famous building in New York City. It seems funny to see a gorilla climbing the building, but a long time ago there was a movie about a gorilla named King Kong, and in that movie he scales the Empire State Building. That means he climbs up the side of that skyscraper.

Yes, *C* is for *colors*.

This board with all the colors on it is called a palette. Artists put different colors of paint on a palette and mix them together to create just the right shades for their paintings. Do you know the names of all the colors on this palette?

◆ Continue sharing the remaining pages. Take the time to share information about all the items presented, encouraging children's responses and questions. In this one very simple alphabet book you will have the opportunity to talk to children about chicks hatching, frogs eating flies, cars needing gas, hot dogs with condiments, ice melting, jack-in-the-boxes, the character Pinocchio, desert scenes, the role of umpires, spider webs, xylophones, and yo-yos. You will also have the opportunity to share the names of specific kitchen utensils, jazz instruments, ice-cream flavors, and vegetables.

◆ Be sure to comment on the illustrations as well, pointing out the vibrant colors and the tiny dots and interesting lines that appear on almost every page.

## TIPS TO CONSIDER

◆ If children err in naming the object selected for a particular letter, be sure to comment on their thinking and gently suggest the author's intention. For example, for the letter *D* Rachel Isadora presents a dancer. If children call out "ballerina," your comments might include the following:

Yes she looks a bit like a ballerina, but ballerina would have to be on the *B* page.

The author wrote "dancer," because this is the *D* page and dancer begins with the /d/ sound. We use the letter *D* to make that sound. In this book, we can say *D* is for *dancer*.

Yours was a good guess because a ballerina is a kind of dancer. This dancer is actually a tap dancer. Look at her shoes. Rachel Isadora even wrote "Tap, Tap, Tap" at the bottom of the page.

◆ Encourage children to call out other words that begin with each letter of the alphabet.

Yes, you're right. In this book *R* is for *rattle*, but in other alphabet books *R* might be for *rabbit* or *rocket*.

◆ Encourage children to announce the names of friends or family members that begin with the letter *R* and the /r/ sound.

## POSSIBILITIES TO EXTEND THE LEARNING

• Share other alphabet books. Ask your librarian to help you choose ones that tap into your children's current interests.

• Share alphabet books with longer passages for each letter of the alphabet. These might include *Animal Alphabet* by Margriet Ruurs, *Appaloosa Zebra: A Horse Lover's Alphabet* by Jesse Haas, and *Ellsworth's Extraordinary Electric Ears* by Valorie Fisher. Read and enjoy each book. After you have reread the book several times, ask children to listen for all the words on each page that begin with the sound of the selected letter.

# 25. Alphabet Search

*ACCOMPLISHMENTS: recognizing and recalling letters of the alphabet, learning sound-symbol correspondence*

This treasure hunt activity helps children recognize and recall letters of the alphabet as well as connect those letters with the beginning sounds of words. The game also requires children to remember the sequence of letters in our alphabet and to pay attention to the names of items in the home or school environment. It is appropriate for children aged 3 and up who show an interest in the names of letters and the sounds they represent.

## MATERIALS TO GATHER

This game requires a stack of sticky notes, a marker, and a wide variety of household items, one per letter. As you write one letter of the alphabet on each note (26 of them), explain to children that you will be using the notes to play a game with them when they awake from their naps or return to their classroom after recess. While children are asleep or away, place letters on appropriate items throughout the house, apartment, or classroom.

A possible household letter-item list follows:

| | | | | |
|---|---|---|---|---|
| A: Air conditioner | G: Gloves | M: Mirror | S: Sofa | Y: Yarn |
| B: Bed | H: Hammer | N: Newspaper | T: Television | Z: Zipper |
| C: Cabinet | I: Ice cube tray | O: Olives | U: Umbrella | |
| D: Door | J: Jar | P: Pillow | V: Vase | |
| E: Eraser | K: Kitchen counter | Q: Quilt | W: Window | |
| F: Frame | L: Lamp | R: Refrigerator | X: Xylophone | |

A possible classroom letter-item list follows:

| | | | | |
|---|---|---|---|---|
| A: Alphabet chart | G: Globe | M: Marker | S: Scissors | Y: Yellow paint |
| B: Bookcase | H: Hexagon | N: Note | T: Tape | Z: Zoo animal |
| C: Clock | I: Ink | O: Octagon | U: Uppercase letter | |
| D: Desk | J: Jump rope | P: Pencil | V: Vent | |
| E: Easel | K: Key | Q: Question mark | W: Windowsill | |
| F: Fishbowl | L: Light | R: Ruler | X: Xylophone | |

## INVITATIONS TO PLAY

◆ Introduce the activity.

Remember all those sticky notes you saw me write? I have placed each one in a very special place. Let's look around and I'll show you what I mean.

Here on the air conditioner, do you see one of the yellow sticky notes? Which letter is on it? That's right, it's an *A*.

I put an *A* there because *air conditioner* starts with an /a/ sound and we use the letter *A* to spell the word *air*.

◆ Continue searching together.

> Let's try and find the next letter of the alphabet together.
>
> What letter comes after *A*? Let's sing the alphabet song to remind us.

◆ Sing the alphabet song together.

> Yes, we need to find the *B*. Where could it be?
>
> What things around us begin with the /b/ sound?
>
> Yes, *B* can be for *book* and *B* can be for *bicycle*, but there are no sticky notes on those.
>
> Let's keep looking. Remember, we are looking for a *B*. Do you remember what a *B* looks like?

Draw another letter *B* on an extra sticky note if children need to see it.

> Yes, you found it right there on the bed. *Bed* begins with the /b/ sound.

◆ Continue the alphabet search, highlighting the names of the items that begin with each letter.

## TIPS TO CONSIDER

◆ Children will spot other sticky notes as they search for letters. You can let them collect them out of order, but if you do, you might suggest that they stick them on a blank wall space in alphabetical order so they can tell which ones are missing. Children will probably need adult guidance to complete the alphabet in order.

◆ Some items will be hard to find, like those inside the refrigerator. Be prepared to give hints.

> For the letter *O*, we will have to search in the refrigerator. Let me open the door for you. Do you see a sticky note?

◆ Children may be so determined to find the sticky notes that they may disregard where they found them. Be prepared to slow them down.

> Where did you find the *C*? Do you know why I put it on the cabinet?

◆ Sticky notes may not adhere for a very long time to some fabrics or may fall down due to air movements. Be prepared to rehang notes on occasion and try to avoid surfaces that they do not adhere to well.

◆ Keep all notes at or below children's eye level so they are easy to find.

◆ If this activity is carried out with a classroom of children, invite an individual child to search for a few letters and then pass the challenge on to another student while classmates watch.

## POSSIBILITIES TO EXTEND THE LEARNING

• Photograph items chosen and make personal alphabet books for children.

• Reverse roles, asking children to place sticky notes on appropriate items.

• Add names of items to sticky notes to build sight vocabulary for 5- and 6-year-olds.

- Include uppercase and lowercase letters on sticky notes.

- Play I Spy in different rooms of the house or areas of the school, offering meaning clues as well as those that suggest sound-symbol correspondence. For example, in the kitchen, you might say the following:

    I am looking at something that begins with the /w/ sound, as in the word *window*.
    We spell that sound with the letter *W*.
    You usually eat it for breakfast.
    Some people like it for a treat with ice cream on it.
    Others prefer it with maple syrup.
    And it is usually has a design on it made up of little squares.
    That's right—I am looking at a waffle.

- Play Touch and Tell by cutting a hole in a carton that is large enough for children to slip their hands in and out. (Cartons from disposable diapers work very well.) Place items in the carton that begin with a selected letter. For example, you might place a small plastic jack-o'-lantern, some jacks, and a jump rope in the box. Then say, "I have three items in the box that begin with the letter *J*, making the sound of /j/ as in *jelly*." Invite children to reach into the box, feel around, and try to guess what you have hidden.

- Play Shoe Bag Sort by labeling pockets of clear plastic shoe bags with letters of the alphabet. Use permanent markers to write big, bold letters. Invite children to find small toys to place in each pocket, choosing ones whose beginning sound matches the letter printed on the pocket. For example, a monkey finger puppet can be placed in the pocket labeled *M*, a top in the *T* pouch, a zebra figurine in the *Z* pocket. Talk about which pockets are hard to fill. Empty all the pockets and ask children to return items to the correct pockets.

- Invite children to plan meals around chosen letter sounds. Serve waffles and watermelon for breakfast (/w/), spaghetti and spinach for lunch (/s/), and turkey, tortellini, and tomatoes for dinner (/t/).

- Using chalk, write the letters of the alphabet in order on the sidewalk. Space them to create a long path. Standing on the *A*, ask children to jump as far as they can, announcing a word that begins with each letter they land on. Continue until children reach the *Z*.

- See Songs With a Twist, on page 79.

- Children also learn to connect letters with the sounds they represent when they are invited to use invented spelling and compose original writing (see pages 127–144).

# SINGING

## 26. Songs to Draw

*ACCOMPLISHMENTS: listening for details, memorizing songs, expanding vocabulary*

This activity involves drawing pictures to accompany carefully selected songs. If children are able, they can do the drawing; if not, they can learn to listen for specific details in the songs and watch as the adult does the illustrating. This activity helps children learn the words to songs, increases youngsters' vocabulary, and provides opportunities for children to listen for specific details. Singing is appropriate for children of all ages. In fact, young children learn a great deal about the sounds of language through song. Children older than 3 can be invited to do the drawing.

## MATERIALS TO GATHER

In addition to art supplies, such as paper and crayons or markers, this activity requires selecting songs that lend themselves to illustration. The lyrics should contain rich details of people, animals, or objects, the kind that appeal to young children. The following sample uses the children's song "Akin Drum."

## INVITATIONS TO PLAY

◆ Sing the song with children.

Do you remember that song called "Akin Drum"? Let's sing it together.

There was a man lived on the moon, lived on the moon, lived on the moon,
There was a man lived on the moon and his name was Akin Drum.

And his hair was made of spaghetti, spaghetti, spaghetti,
And his hair was made of spaghetti and his name was Akin Drum.

◆ Continue with such lyrics as "And his eyes were made of meatballs" and "And he played upon a ladle."

Can you picture someone who lives upon the moon?

Can you imagine someone whose hair is made of spaghetti?

Can you picture someone whose eyes are made of meatballs?

Can you picture someone playing upon a ladle? A ladle is a big spoon we use to scoop soup from a pot. Can you show him playing upon a ladle?

Maybe we could draw a picture of Akin Drum and see if our friends can guess the song from our picture.

How would you draw someone who lives on the moon?

Can you make hair that looks like spaghetti?

How would meatball eyes look?

- If children are not ready to draw such precise things or choose not to draw, try your own hand at illustrating. Children will delight in seeing your artwork. Of course, you can work together on the illustration. (See child's illustration at right.)

- Have children display their work, suggesting they ask visitors or family members to guess the titles from the illustrations.

    When Grandma comes over, we'll see if she recognizes the song from our picture.

## TIPS TO CONSIDER

- "Akin Drum" is a popular children's song with many versions. If you are unfamiliar with it, borrow a recording from your local library or find one online. Add additional body parts and funny foods, making up verses as you go. For example,

Akin Drum's neck can be made of string beans, his chin can be made of gumdrops, his arms can be made of Jell-O, and his feet can be made of pizza. The possibilities are limitless.

## POSSIBILITIES TO EXTEND THE LEARNING

- Borrow recordings of other children's songs from your public library or find them online. Use these to recall familiar songs and to learn new ones. Listen for ones that can be easily illustrated.

- Illustrations can be made from many other popular children's songs and rhymes, including "Miss Mary Mack," "I'm a Little Teapot," and "There Was a Crooked Man." Illustrations can also be made from novelty rock-and-roll songs, such as "The Purple People Eater" and "Itsy Bitsy Teenie Weenie Yellow Polka Dot Bikini." Be sure to play and sing these songs frequently and joyously for children before asking them to illustrate.

- You can teach children some of your favorite old songs and have them illustrate the titles, a few lines, or even entire lyrics in a picture book format. Suggested songs include "Tiptoe Through the Tulips" and "Raindrops Keep Falling on My Head."

- Use illustrations to play Name That Tune, in which children ask family members to figure out the song just from the drawing. They take great delight when family members guess correctly and even more when they are stumped. Be sure to sing the songs each time.

- Borrow from the library songs that have been published in picture book format, including those by Raffi, Tom Paxton, and even Billy Joel. Read the words, talk about the illustrations, and most of all, sing the songs frequently and with gusto.

- Share collections of children's songs that are accompanied by famous works of arts. These include Shona McKellar's *A Child's Book of Lullabies,* with paintings by Mary Cassatt, and *Go In and Out the Window: An Illustrated Songbook for Young People* by Dan Fox.

# 27. Songs With a Twist

*ACCOMPLISHMENTS: developing sound-symbol correspondence, playing with words, expanding vocabulary*

Children learn a great deal by listening to songs over and over again and singing them as well. In this activity, children delight in being surprised when a song they know well takes on a new twist. In other words, they roar with laughter when the adult singer changes the words "by mistake."

In the examples that follow, children learn to choose words that begin with selected letters, play with words, and increase their vocabulary. This activity is appropriate for children aged 2½ and up, or once children know the words to the traditional songs and rhymes.

## MATERIALS TO GATHER

All that is required is a knowledge of the words and tunes to popular children's songs. Then with a little imagination and a sense of humor, you can surprise young listeners with some funny substitutions. Several examples follow.

## INVITATIONS TO PLAY

◆ Introduce the activity.

Let's sing the alphabet song, you know, the one that ends with "Now I know my ABCs/Next time won't you sing with me?"

◆ Sing the song traditionally with children and then offer to perform alone.

Now I am going to sing it all by myself. See if I do a good job.
A-B-C-D / E-F-G / H-I-J-K / L-M-N-O . . . Pizza!

◆ Be prepared for children to laugh, correct you, shriek "Noooo!" or comment on how silly you are. Try it again, this time offering *pretzel* instead of the letter *P*. Continue with other irresistible words beginning with the /p/ sound (*pumpkin, popcorn, pineapple, pickle*). Don't be surprised if the children catch on and offer their own favorite *P* words. Words, of course, need not be foods.

◆ Introduce another song.

How about singing "She'll Be Coming 'Round the Mountain"?

First sing the song traditionally.

She'll be coming 'round the mountain when she comes. (Toot! Toot!)
She'll be coming 'round the mountain when she comes. (Toot! Toot!)
She'll be coming 'round the mountain.
She'll be coming 'round the mountain.
She'll be coming 'round the mountain when she comes. (Toot! Toot!)

◆ Then offer to sing the song again, this time substituting surprising places for "the mountain."

She'll be coming 'round the bathroom when she comes.

- Expect children to laugh and correct you.

    Okay, how about, "She'll be coming 'round the kitchen when she comes"?

    Okay, I'll get it straight this time. How's this—"She'll be coming 'round the basement when she comes"?

- Try substituting other places familiar to the children, not simply rooms in the home.

    She'll be coming 'round Grand Central when she comes.

    She'll be coming 'round Riverside Park when she comes.

- If children remain engaged, introduce another song with a twist.

    Let's sing "If You're Happy and You Know It." As we sing, we are going to do all the things we sing about, like clapping our hands and stomping our feet.

- Sing the song traditionally with children.

    If you're happy and you know it, clap your hands.

    If you're happy and you know it, clap your hands.

    If you're happy and you know it, then your face should surely show it.

    If you're happy and you know it, clap your hands.

- Continue singing, substituting "stomp your feet" for "clap your hands."

- Continue singing, substituting "shout Hurray!" for "stomp your feet."

- Continue singing, ending with "do all three!"

- Next, expand children's vocabulary by including such commands as "scratch your chin," "pinch your cheek," and "wiggle your ear." Demonstrate the meaning of each command, inviting children to follow the direction. Then end with "do all three!"

- Create new verses, adding such sets of commands as:

    "mess up your hair," "curl your tongue," "wink your eyes"

    "puff your cheeks," "stick out your tongue," "raise your eyebrows"

    "wriggle your nose," "purse your lips," "nod your head"

    "tilt your head," "blink your eyes," "sniff your nose"

    "pat your nose," "rub your forehead," "tickle your neck"

## TIPS TO CONSIDER

- Some children get upset if you vary their favorite familiar tunes. Be prepared to postpone innovations if children are not ready.

- If any of the songs or rhymes noted here are unfamiliar to you or you have forgotten some of their lines or their tunes, ask a public librarian to lend you a copy of the verses as well as a recording of the songs.

## POSSIBILITIES TO EXTEND THE LEARNING

- You can vary the twist on the alphabet song by selecting different letters to play around with. For example, instead of announcing the letter *L*, suggest "lollipop," "lemonade," or "lunchtime." Instead of the letter *S*, suggest "sandwich," "scooter" or "summertime." Invite children to add their own substitutions.

- Make surprising changes to phrases in other verses of "She'll be Coming 'Round the Mountain." For example, instead of "She'll be driving six white horses when she comes," you could substitute, "six yellow taxis." Instead of "Then we'll all have chicken and dumplings when she comes," you could surprise young listeners with "spaghetti and meatballs."

- Vary the emotions in "If You're Happy and You Know It." Try singing, "If you're sad and you know it" or "If you're scared and you know it."

- Add surprising twists to other favorite and familiar songs or rhymes. For example, have Humpty Dumpty sit on something other than a wall, the Itsy Bitsy Spider climb up something other than the waterspout, and Jack and Jill fetch something other than a pail of water.

# 28. Songs and Rhymes Personalized

*ACCOMPLISHMENTS: memorizing verses, rhyming words, following instructions, playing with language*

Many grown-ups sing the traditional lines "Rain, rain, go away. Come again some other day" as children gaze longingly out rain-streaked windows. It comes naturally to fill in your own child's name when the verse continues, "Little Zachary wants to play." In the activity that follows, other traditional songs and rhymes are personalized, using the names and favorite possessions of the children in your care. Throughout, children have opportunities to memorize verses, rhyme words, practice counting, follow instructions, play with language, and anticipate endings. This activity is appropriate for all ages.

## MATERIALS TO GATHER

If you are familiar with many children's songs and rhymes, no additional materials are required. If children's songs are new for you or you need to brush up on popular ones, ask your librarian for collections of traditional songs, rhymes, and finger plays. Compact discs or cassette tapes often accompany these books. You can also find recordings of traditional children's songs online.

## INVITATIONS TO PLAY

◆ Share songs, finger plays, or rhymes throughout the day. Some will be especially handy on long car or bus rides ("Ten in the Bed"). Others will work best when cuddling on the couch ("This Little Piggy"). Some might help distract children who don't like to get dressed ("One, Two, Buckle My Shoe"). Others might be perfect for children who need to work off lots of extra energy ("The Hokey Pokey"). The traditional versions should be sung before the personalized ones.

  Do you remember the song that begins "There were ten in the bed, and the little one said, 'Roll over, roll over'"?

◆ Continue singing the song, asking children to join in.
  So they all rolled over and one fell out.
  There were nine in the bed
  And the little one said, "Roll over, roll over."

◆ Continue singing, decreasing the number each time one falls out.
  So they all rolled over and one fell out.
  There were eight in the bed . . ."

◆ Continue singing until only one is left, concluding with "Good night."
  There was one in the bed
  And the little one said, "Good night."

◆ Now personalize the song.

This time when I sing the song, I am going to use one of your names instead of saying "the little one."

◆ If a child's name is a short one, like Ben, add syllables by singing, "And little Ben said, 'Roll over, roll over.'"

◆ Sing the song in its entirety, substituting the child's name.

◆ Sing it again with the name of another child.

◆ Add another innovation to the song by switching the verbs (action words).

This time when I sing the song, I am going to use your name again, but I am not going to say "Roll over." Instead, I am going to use different words.

◆ Invite children to do the actions as you sing.

There were ten in the bed

And little Will said, "Jump over, jump over."

◆ Sing the entire song using the word *jump*, and then try it with other verbs including *slide*, *hop*, *scoot*, *slither*, *skip*, and *bounce*.

## TIPS TO CONSIDER

◆ Some children might not want you to change a single word of their favorite songs. Postpone this activity until they are ready.

◆ Listen to recordings of the songs if their tunes are unfamiliar.

◆ Let children choose names to use if they do not want to use their own.

Who shall we sing about this time?

### POSSIBILITIES TO EXTEND THE LEARNING

• Think through other songs, rhymes, and finger plays that can be personalized. Invite children to sing the song in its traditional format and then sing it again substituting familiar names. A few examples follow.

• As you recite the traditional rhyme "This Little Piggy Went to Market," count the child's toes. Tickle the child's whole body as you say the last line.

This little piggy went to market.

This little piggy stayed home.

This little piggy ate roast beef.

This little piggy had none.

And this little piggy cried, "Wee, wee, wee," all the way home.

Then personalize the finger play by selecting names of siblings, cousins, or friends.

Our friend Sasha went to market.

Our friend Zach stayed home.

Our friend Will had roast beef.

Our friend Ben had none.

And our friend Andie cried, "Wee, wee, wee," all the way home.

Alternate names so that the same child isn't always the one to cry or get none. Or, you can, substitute "ice-cream cone" for "none," or a child's favorite food for "roast beef." You can also personalize the rhyme by using the name of your neighborhood food store instead of "market."

- When you share the "Pat-a-Cake" rhyme, try substituting a child's name for "baby." This works especially well if the child's name begins with a letter that rhymes with the word *me*.

Here is the traditional verse:

Pat-a-Cake, pat-a-cake, baker's man,

Bake me a cake as fast as you can,

Roll it and pat it and mark it with a B,

And put it in the oven for baby and me.

Here is a personalized ending:

. . . mark it with a D,

And put it in the oven for Daniella and me.

Any name beginning with the following letters will fit the rhyming pattern: *B, C, D, E, G, P, T, V,* and *Z.* For names beginning with other letters, use the alternate ending:

. . . mark it with glee,

And put it in the oven for Kevin and me.

- Do "The Hokey Pokey" with the name of children's favorite things, inviting them to hold each item and shake it all about.

You put your teddy bear in,

You put your teddy bear out,

You put your teddy bear in,

And you shake it all about.

You do the hokey pokey,

And you turn yourself around,

That's what it's all about.

Continue singing, referring to other beloved items ("You put your green sweatshirt in . . .").

- Share the popular rhyme "One, Two, Buckle Your Shoe."

  One, two, buckle your shoe.

  Three, four, shut the door.

  Five, six, pick up sticks.

  Seven, eight, lay them straight.

  Nine, ten, a big fat hen.

Personalize the rhyme, referring to children's interests.

  One, two, Will wants to go to the zoo.

  Three, four, he wants the lion to roar.

  Five, six, he wants the monkey to do tricks.

  Seven, eight, hurry, don't be late!

  Nine, ten, Will says, "Let's go there again!"

You can also personalize the rhyme by referring to familiar local landmarks.

  One, two, let's go to the Bronx Zoo.

  Three, four, let's take the Circle Line tour.

  Five, six, let's root for the Knicks.

  Seven, eight, let's drive upstate.

  Nine, ten, let's start over again!

- Borrow *My Aunt Came Back* by Pat Cummings. Create additional lines referring to places that the children know.

  My aunt came back from Old New York, and she brought with her a pound of pork.

  My aunt came back from Chinatown, and she brought with her a laughing clown.

  My aunt came back from the Empire State, and she brought with her an iron gate.

# 29. Old Songs, New Versions

*ACCOMPLISHMENTS: playing with language, appreciating rhymes,
learning new vocabulary and concepts, memorizing songs*

In Songs With a Twist (page 79) we surprised children by adding a twist in the middle of a familiar song. In Songs and Rhymes Personalized (page 82) we personalized familiar songs or rhymes by adding children's names or favorite things. Here we will be singing familiar songs and then creating entirely new versions or adding new stanzas. These types of activities allow children to play with language, appreciate rhymes, learn new vocabulary and concepts, and memorize songs. This activity is appropriate for all ages.

## MATERIALS TO GATHER

This activity requires no materials if you are familiar with traditional childhood songs, but you do need to think of new ways to present them. The examples that follow will suggest possibilities and serve as models as you create your own versions. If necessary, refresh your memory by borrowing books or recordings from your library.

## INVITATIONS TO PLAY

◆ Begin by singing the traditional version of "The Farmer in the Dell."

> The farmer in the dell,
> The farmer in the dell,
> Hi-ho, the derry-o!
> The farmer in the dell.

◆ Continue singing, adding the following traditional lines.

> The farmer takes a wife . . .
> The wife takes a child . . .
> The child takes a nurse . . .
> The nurse takes a dog . . .
> The dog takes a cat . . .
> The cat takes a rat . . .
> The rat takes the cheese . . .
> The cheese stands alone.

◆ Now use the tune to sing about animals in the jungle.

> Now I am going to teach you a new song that will remind you of "The Farmer in the Dell," but it is about animals in the jungle.

◆ Share the following song with the children.

> The lion in the jungle,
> The lion in the jungle,

Hi-ho, the derry-o!

The lion in the jungle.

◆ Continue singing, adding the following lines.

The lion takes a hyena,

The lion takes a hyena,

Hi-ho, the derry-o!

The lion takes a hyena.

◆ Continue with the following lines.

The hyena takes a crocodile . . .

The crocodile takes a snake . . .

The snake takes a lizard . . .

The lizard takes a frog . . .

The frog takes a fly . . .

The fly stands alone.

◆ Introduce other songs if children are still engaged (see Possibilities to Extend the Learning for suggestions).

## TIPS TO CONSIDER

◆ Stick to original words if children are reluctant to vary their favorite tunes or rhymes.

◆ Play recordings of traditional songs frequently so that children can recall the melodies.

## POSSIBILITIES TO EXTEND THE LEARNING

• Create new versions for other traditional songs and poems. Examples follow.

• Sing "Head, Shoulders, Knees, and Toes" in the traditional way, encouraging children to touch matching body parts as they are called out.

Head, shoulders, knees and toes, knees and toes.

Head, shoulders, knees and toes, knees and toes.

Eyes and ears and mouth and nose.

Head, shoulders, knees and toes, knees and toes.

Then challenge children to touch different body parts as you sing the following versions.

Arms, fingers, mouth and teeth, mouth and teeth.

Arms, fingers, mouth and teeth, mouth and teeth.

Chin and forehead, legs and feet.

Arms, fingers, mouth and teeth, mouth and teeth.

Thumbs, elbows, back and thighs, back and thighs.

Thumbs, elbows, back and thighs, back and thighs.

Neck and hair and lips and eyes.

Thumbs, elbows, back and thighs, back and thighs.

- Sing the traditional words to "The Wheels on the Bus."

    The wheels on the bus go round and round,

    Round and round, round and round.

    The wheels on the bus go round and round,

    All through the town.

    Continue singing using the following traditional lines.

    The driver on the bus says, "Move on back."

    The people on the bus go up and down.

    The babies on the bus go, "Wah, wah, wah."

    The mommies on the bus go, "Shh, shh, shh."

    The money on the bus goes clink, clink, clink.

    The wipers on the bus go swish, swish, swish.

    The horn on the bus goes beep, beep, beep.

    Create new verses for "The Wheels on the Bus" by adding community workers as passengers.

    The police officer on the bus says, "Hold on tight."

    The teacher on the bus says, "Read a good book."

    The firefighter on the bus says, "Never play with matches."

    The doctor on the bus says, "Take your vitamins."

    Or invite animals onto the bus.

    The dog on the bus goes, "Bow, wow, wow."

    The pig on the bus goes, "Oink, oink, oink."

    The horse on the bus goes, "Neigh, neigh, neigh."

    The cat on the bus goes, "Meow, meow, meow."

    You can even invite the children's pop culture friends to board the bus.

    Dora on the bus says, "Hola, amigo."

    Diego on the bus says, "Adios, amigo."

    Bob the Builder on the bus says, "I can fix it."

- Invite children to create their own lines for "The Wheels on the Bus."

- Share the following childhood rhyme with children.

    I love you once, I love you twice,

I love you more than beans and rice.

Create additional rhyming verses, explaining the meaning of any unfamiliar terms.

I love you once, I love you twice,
I love you more than good advice.

I love you once, I love you twice,
I love you more than cinnamon spice.

I love you once, I love you twice,
I love you more than cats love mice.

I love you once, I love you twice,
I love you more than a strawberry ice.

I love you once, I love you twice,
I love you more than a pizza slice.

I love you once, I love you twice,
I love you more than a bargain price.

- Ask librarians to help you discover picture books that are takeoffs or versions of classic songs and rhymes. These include *Old MacDonald Had a Woodshop* by Lisa Shulman, *I Ain't Gonna Paint No More!* by Karen Beaumont, and *I Know an Old Lady Who Swallowed a Pie* by Alison Jackson. Be sure to share the traditional song or rhyme before sharing the takeoffs.

# VOCABULARY AND CONCEPTS

## 30. Neighborhood Tours

*ACCOMPLISHMENTS: learning to use a field guide, expanding vocabulary and concepts, matching pictures to real-life objects*

Young children delight in figuring out how things work and in knowing the names of everything in their environment. In this activity, children are encouraged to carry a children's guidebook as they take a walking or stroller tour of their neighborhood. Here, neighborhood dogs are the main topic of interest. Children learn the names of various kinds of dogs, expanding their vocabulary and strengthening their ability to note details. They also learn to appreciate guidebooks as an important reference tool. This activity is appropriate for all children who show an interest in looking at pictures and matching those to real-life plants, animals, or objects.

## MATERIALS TO GATHER

This activity requires a children's field guide, presenting the precise names of things found in the children's neighborhood. In other words, a guide to trees, birds, vehicles, insects, clouds, flowers, and so on would be appropriate. Here, the beautiful and inviting book *Dog* by Matthew Van Fleet, with photographs by Brian Stanton, is used. See Possibilities to Extend the Learning for more suggestions.

## INVITATIONS TO PLAY

◆ Share the book *Dog* with the children, encouraging the children to touch the varying textures, shift the parts that move, and fold out the surprising final page. Be sure to probe their understanding of all the interesting adjectives (describing words) and verbs (action words) included in this text. Above all, engage children in conversations about the various breeds of dog, asking them about their likes and dislikes.

Do you know anything else that is fluffy? Scruffy? Droopy? Perky?

When are you neat? When are you sloppy?

What else in your house feels silky? Shaggy? Soft?

Do you know what *quake* means?

Do you know any other animals that drool, pant, and slobber?

What else looks smooth? What else looks curly?

Do you bark, howl, or sniff?

*Plain* and *fancy* are opposites. Have you ever eaten a plain meal? A fancy one? Have you ever worn a plain outfit? A fancy one?

Why do you think this one is called a chocolate Labrador?

Which would you rather have, a dachshund or a golden retriever?

Which dog looks like the one that lives across the hall?

Have you ever seen a dog in the neighborhood that looks like that one?

Which would you rather take for a walk, a pug or a poodle?

Let's take the book outside with us today. We can try to find different kinds of dogs.

◆ When you spot a dog, stop to observe it. Ask the children if the dog looks like any in the book.

◆ If the dog and its owner or walker seem approachable, ask the breed of the dog.

◆ Look up the breed in the book, showing the children the similarities between the picture and the dog.

◆ At the end of the stroll, tally the number and breeds of dogs seen.

Well, today we saw two pugs, one poodle, and one dachshund.

◆ Encourage children to share their discoveries with friends or family members.

## TIPS TO CONSIDER

◆ Make sure children keep their distance from unfamiliar dogs. Young children's abrupt movements and shrill voices can startle an otherwise friendly dog.

◆ Never let children approach strangers. Grown-ups should initiate all conversations.

◆ Demonstrate polite ways to approach a stranger when you're asking for information.

◆ Some adult guidebooks present helpful labeled photographs but contain too much information for young children. When you're using these books, you can refer only to the photos and their captions.

## POSSIBILITIES TO EXTEND THE LEARNING

• Take strolls with other guides in hand, selecting those topics that are of interest to your children. A few possibilities follow:

*Beachcombing: Exploring the Seashore* by Jim Arnosky

*Bugs, Bugs, Bugs* by Bob Barner

*Take a Tree Walk* by Jane Kirkland

*The Wonder Book of Flowers* by Cynthia Iliff Koehler

• Photograph items or animals spotted. Then help children create their own neighborhood guidebooks.

• Read additional nonfiction books on the children's areas of interest. (See Finding Five on page 17.)

# 31. New Words Naturally

*ACCOMPLISHMENTS: expanding vocabulary, describing events*

Children with large vocabularies, those who understand and use a wide range of words in the early years, are quite likely to become successful readers and writers when they begin school. In this activity, you will be offering young children opportunities to expand their vocabularies naturally and joyfully by immersing them in many ways of describing events. This activity is appropriate for all children aged 2 to 6.

## MATERIALS TO GATHER

This activity requires no special materials. To prepare, simply think about the situations that recur for you and your children each day and think about the words you choose to describe, explain, or comment on those events. Try to use words with similar or related meanings whenever possible. Several examples follow.

## INVITATIONS TO PLAY

◆ As you and your children toss and catch a Frisbee, comment on each throw in a variety of ways.

> It's soaring in the sky.
> It's rocketing over the clouds.
> It's flying high.
> It's zooming through the air.
> It's sailing over our heads.
> It's twirling in the air.
> It's speeding through the atmosphere.

(Don't hesitate to use big words like *atmosphere* with young children. They catch on rather quickly.)

◆ As you and your children eat lunch, offer comments throughout the meal.

> Let's begin eating together.
> You're really munching that carrot.
> Make sure you are chewing your chicken patty carefully.
> Be careful that you are not swallowing very big pieces.
> Wow, you must really be hungry, you're really devouring those chicken nuggets.
> Are you still nibbling on that celery stalk?
> Whoa, slow down. I think you are gulping down that apple juice too quickly.

◆ When they taste something especially good, use several different describing words (adjectives).

> Do you think it's delicious?
> I think it's yummy.
> I wonder if it is nutritious.
> Your brother also thinks it's delectable.

This is the tastiest dessert I have ever had.

It's simply scrumptious.

◆ When they create a big block construction, offer several compliments.

It's gigantic!

I didn't know you could build such a huge construction.

It's not just big, it's colossal!

It's the most enormous building you have ever made.

This is an immense structure!

◆ When they are deciding on a toy to play with, think aloud using different action words (verbs).

I wonder which one you'll select.

I can't wait to see which one you'll choose.

I hope you pick one I can play with too.

◆ When playing hide-and-seek, you can offer a few million-dollar words.

It seems like you've really disappeared.

I can't find you—it's as if you've vanished into thin air.

You have really concealed yourself this time.

I hope I can discover your hiding place.

Have you become invisible? I *really* can't see you.

This is a mystery. I don't have a clue about your whereabouts.

It's as if you've left without a trace.

◆ When children get hurt, you can describe the incident in many ways.

Oh, no! You got a boo-boo.

You really got hurt.

I am sorry that you got scraped.

Looks like you injured your knee.

I hope you don't fall down again.

Be careful not to trip.

Uh-oh! Looks like you stumbled again.

Please don't take any more tumbles.

I once stubbed my toe doing that!

## TIPS TO CONSIDER

◆ Use words naturally, trusting that children will usually be able to understand their meaning from the context of the situation.

◆ Do not expect children to use all of the new words on their own immediately, but take great delight when the words do appear.

## POSSIBILITIES TO EXTEND THE LEARNING

- Read aloud Audrey Wood's *The Napping House*, a book that contains many words related to sleeping, including *dozing, dreaming, snoring, napping, sleeping, slumbering,* and *snoozing.* Talk to children about the differences in meaning between the words. (This popular book should be readily available in most public libraries.)

- Gather additional picture books that contain many precise verbs and share them with children. For example, you can point out the meaning of all the interesting ways animals make sounds in Bill Martin, Jr., and Eric Carle's *Polar Bear, Polar Bear, What Do You Hear?*

- Point out all the ways that birds move in Joanne Ryder's *Wild Birds.*

- Point out all the ways the members of a family behave in Jane Kurtz's *Rain Romp: Stomping Away a Grouchy Day.*

- Point out all the ways the animals behave and move in Karma Wilson's *Bear Snores On.*

- Point out all the sophisticated adjectives in Eric Carle's *"Slowly, Slowly, Slowly," Said the Sloth.*

- Point out the specific names of baby animals in *A Pinky Is a Baby Mouse* by Pam Muñoz Ryan, John Graham's *A Crowd of Cows,* and *Kangaroos Have Joeys* by Philippa-Alys Browne.

- Share Jane O'Connor's *Fancy Nancy* and *Fancy Nancy and the Posh Puppy*, stories about a young girl who delights in using "fancy" words.

- Borrow a children's thesaurus from the library for additional ideas. Look up such child-friendly words as *shine, laugh,* and *great.* Weave the words you find (*sparkle, chuckle, terrific,* and so on) into your conversations with youngsters.

# WORD STUDY

## 32. Silly Sandwich Syllable Strings

*ACCOMPLISHMENTS: recognizing syllables, expanding vocabulary*

This game introduces the idea that words can be broken up into separate "sound parts" called syllables. It also introduces names of new foods and encourages conversation about the making of sandwiches. This activity will lead to lots of laughter as well as shrieks of "Yucky!" It is appropriate for children aged 3½ and up, once children can count to five and understand the meaning of each number.

### MATERIALS TO GATHER

This activity requires very little preparation and no materials. It is therefore a great way to pass the time in a doctor's waiting room or on a long car or bus ride, or in the school cafeteria as children wait for their table to be called.

### INVITATIONS TO PLAY

◆ Introduce the concept of syllables.

> Did you realize that words are made up of different parts? Some words have only one part, but others have two, three, four, or even five parts. These parts are called syllables.

◆ Clap once, then twice, then three times, then four, and then five, each time asking how many beats the children heard.

> Listen to me clap and tell me how many claps you hear.

◆ Say each child's name, clearly breaking the name into parts and clapping out the syllables.

> Now I am going to clap as I say your name.
>
> *An-die* (accompanied by two claps).
>
> How many times did I clap? How many syllables do you hear?

◆ Say and clap out other family names.

> *Zach-a-ry* (three claps).
>
> *Will* (one clap).
>
> *Ben-ja-min* (three claps).
>
> *Shel-ley* (two claps).

◆ Once children understand syllables, or parts, the Silly Sandwich game can begin.

> Now, I am going to teach you how to play Silly Sandwich. Let's pretend we are going to make a sandwich. I am going to put the first food in the sandwich. But the food I choose has to be a

one-syllable word.

So I am going to pick *jam*. *Jam* has only one syllable, doesn't it? Let's clap it out. *Jam* (one clap).

Now it's your turn, and you have to pick a food that is a two-syllable word.

◆ Offer some suggestions if children are struggling.

You could choose *ap-ple* or *sar-dines* or *pep-per* or *string-cheese*.

◆ Be accepting if children choose one of your selections and congratulate them if they think of one on their own. For example, a child might suggest *pick-les*.

Great, now our silly sandwich has jam and pickles. And it's my turn to add a food that is a three-syllable word. How about *sa-la-mi*? Would you eat a sandwich with jam, pickles, and salami on it?

Do you want to try and add a food that has four parts in its name, four syllables? Should we add *pea-nut but-ter* to our silly sandwich?

◆ Of course you can stop right here or continue with a five-syllable food, like *choc-o-late pud-ding*.

◆ Start again, creating a whole new silly sandwich.

Do you want to go first with a food that has only one syllable?

◆ Continue playing. The possibilities are endless. A few samples follow:

Salt, lemon, broccoli, Caesar salad, marinara sauce.

Egg, mustard, tomato, watermelon, lemon meringue pie.

Milk, olives, mayonnaise, huckleberries, strawberry shortcake.

## TIPS TO CONSIDER

◆ It might take some children a while to catch on to listening for and counting syllables. If so, postpone the game and just have fun listening to the parts of words. If children show interest, clap out names of foods at each meal to help them understand the idea of syllables.

◆ Begin playing with just one- and two-syllable words, then move on to three syllables and upward.

### POSSIBILITIES TO EXTEND THE LEARNING

• Ask children to create a silly sandwich that he or she would be willing to eat. Then, make the sandwich.

• The game can also be played with names of animals. Children are asked to pick a pet, moving from one-syllable to five-syllable words. A sample syllable string might begin with the one-syllable *cat*, move to *parrot*, then *anteater*, on to *spider monkey*, and finally to the five-syllable *golden retriever*. Discuss with children which ones would make good pets and which ones would not.

Look Who's Learning to Read

# 33. Title Word Count

*ACCOMPLISHMENTS: appreciating titles, understanding that sentences are composed of individual words, listening to read-alouds*

In this simple sorting game, children are asked to sort a stack of books, based on the number of words in the title. In doing so, they become aware of the meaning of the title of a book and become aware of the concept of individual words. At the end of the sorting, the children get to choose the books they want to hear read. This activity is appropriate for children aged 3½ and up. It is not appropriate for children who are as yet unable to count one to four items accurately.

## MATERIALS TO GATHER

Select a short stack of books you plan to read aloud to your children. As you make your choices, be sure that there are varying numbers of words in the titles. Books used here contain one, two, three, or four words. These numbers can also be written on sticky notes to help children as they sort the books.

## INVITATIONS TO PLAY

◆ Introduce the concept of speech and print being made up of separate words.

When we meet people in the street, some folks say, "Hello," and some folks say, "Hi, there!" and sometimes people say, "How are you?" Those are three different ways to greet people.

◆ Hold up the correct number of fingers as you count out the words in the explanation below.

"Hello" is only one word: Hello.

"Hi, there!" is two words: *Hi* and *there*.

And "How are you?" is three words: *How* and *are* and *you*.

◆ Let me think of another way to greet you and you tell me how many words I am saying.

"Good morning!" How many words did I say?

◆ If children are unable to tell you, count the words for them.

*Good* and *morning*. That's two words.

◆ Continue exploring the number of words in phrases with children.

How about if I say, "Hola"? That's Spanish for "hello." Yes, that's only one word: *Hola*.

How about when I am leaving and I say, "See you later"? How many words is that? Yes that's three words: *See* and *you* and *later*.

How about, "See you later, alligator"? Yes, that's four words.

◆ To see if children have an awareness of words, switch to street signs.

You know that when we walk down the street, we pass lots of signs. Some signs say Stop. How many words is that? *Stop*.

Some signs say One Way. How many words is that? *One Way*.

Some signs say Do Not Enter. How many words is that? *Do Not Enter.*

Some signs say Please Curb Your Dog. How many words is that? *Please Curb Your Dog.*

◆ If children seem to need more practice, switch to names. Mention the names of friends, family, or class-mates, being sure to include some with two and some with three names.

How many names do you have? Let's count all your names.

◆ Connect names of people to titles of books.

Just as people have names, so do books. Do you remember what we call the names of books? That's right—titles.

Some titles have only one word, some have two, some have three, and some have four or even more. I have a stack of books right here, and I am going to read the titles to you. Can you tell me how many words are in each title?

◆ Present a stack of books with varying numbers of words in the titles that you are interested in reading aloud. A possible stack follows:

*Caps for Sale* by Esphyr Slobodkina

*Chicka Chicka Boom Boom* by Bill Martin, Jr., and John Archambault

*The Daddy Book* by Ann Morris

*Jamberry* by Bruce Degen

*Knuffle Bunny: A Cautionary Tale* by Mo Willems

*Little Red Monkey* by Jonathan London

*Llama, Llama Red Pajama* by Anna Dewdney

*Mr. Cookie Baker* by Monica Wellington

*Olivia* by Ian Falconer

*Pete's a Pizza* by William Steig

*Please, Baby, Please* by Spike Lee and Tonya Lewis Lee

*Sheep in a Jeep* by Nancy Shaw

*Snowmen at Night* by Caralyn Buehner

*Tanka, Tanka, Skunk!* by Steve Webb

*The Very Hungry Caterpillar* by Eric Carle

◆ Announce each title and ask children how many words are in the title. If children do not catch on, repeat the title slowly, separating each word and holding up a finger as you say each word.

On these little sticky notes I have written the numbers 1, 2, 3, and 4.

I am going to read the titles again, and you can tell me if I should put a 1, 2, 3, or 4 on that book.

How about *Olivia*?

Yes that's a one-word title, so let's put the number 1 on it.

How about *Knuffle Bunny*?

Yes, that's a two-word title, so let's put the number 2 on it.

How about *Little Red Monkey*?

Yes, that has three words, so we will stick the number 3 on it.

How about *Llama, Llama, Red Pajama*?

Yes, that's four words, so we will put the number 4 on it.

◆ Continue with the remaining books, forming stacks of books that have the same number of words in the titles.

◆ If children seem ready, remove sticky notes and have them re-sort the books on their own. Some children may recall the titles, and some may need you to read the words aloud.

◆ Ask children to choose which books you should read aloud and in what order.

## TIPS TO CONSIDER

◆ Don't be surprised if children think that the words *Snowmen* and *Jamberry* should be counted as two words. Accept their smart thinking and do not feel obliged to explain compound words (words made up of two distinct words) to very young children.

◆ For this activity, avoid the subtitle of *Knuffle Bunny: A Cautionary Tale*, as it may complicate the counting.

◆ Do not attempt to read all the books in one sitting. Know your children's limits.

## POSSIBILITIES TO EXTEND THE LEARNING

• Take advantage of other occasions to heighten children's awareness of words. For example, you could talk about the items on your grocery list.

Look at all the things I have written on my shopping list.

Some of them are one-word items, some are two-word items.

Would you like to know what I am going to shop for today?

Share the list with children, commenting on the number of words in each item.

Chocolate syrup. That's two words—*chocolate* and *syrup*.

Peaches. That's one word—*peaches*.

Chicken soup. That's two words—*chicken* and *soup*.

Animal crackers. That's two words—*animal* and *crackers*.

Lettuce. That's only one word—*lettuce*.

If children seem interested and ready, continue reading the shopping list, asking the children to call out the number of words they hear in each item.

Cheddar cheese

Turkey burgers

Milk

Plastic sandwich bags

Strawberry jam

- Similarly, share listings of children's favorite television programs. Read them aloud, asking children how many words are in the names of the programs. You can also show them the printed listings in the newspaper or television guide.

  I am going to read aloud this list of your favorite shows. Tell me how many words you hear in the name of each program.

  *Mickey Mouse Clubhouse*

  *Maisy*

  *I Spy*

  *Blue's Clues*

  *Jack's Big Music Show*

  *Dora the Explorer*

  *Go, Diego, Go!*

  *Sesame Street*

Some children may be ready to attend to the print, noticing the spaces between words. Others may not.

# SIGHT VOCABULARY

# 34. Family Name Fun

*ACCOMPLISHMENTS: recognizing names, developing sight vocabulary, using familiar words to learn new ones*

One of the very first words most children learn to recognize is their own name. This activity, along with those in Possibilities to Extend the Learning, capitalizes on children's fascination with their own names as well as the names of family members and friends. Whenever the opportunity arises, point out the children's names in print, form their names with magnetic letters, write them on steamy windows, spell them out in cupcake icing, build them with alphabet blocks, and so on. Children can then use all the names they recognize to help them learn new words. This activity is appropriate for children aged 3 and up, or whenever children show an interest in seeing names in print.

## MATERIALS TO GATHER

This first name game follows the rules of Go Fish and requires a standard deck of 52 playing cards, a marker, and small stick-on labels or masking tape you can write on. Separate cards by rank (aces with aces and so on), creating 13 piles of four cards each. Select 13 names that have important meaning for each child. You can create separate sets for the child's first name, middle name, and surname, and then select 10 others. Choose from parents, siblings, grandparents, cousins, aunts, uncles, close friends, teachers, and neighbors. Stick labels or strips of tape on the face of each card. Then neatly print one name on all four cards of the same rank. (If you think children won't be able to recognize a name, attach a photo of the person to at least one of the cards as an additional support.)

## INVITATIONS TO PLAY

◆ Review the game Go Fish as described in the box at right and introduce this special version.

 Do you remember how to play Go Fish? Today I

### HOW TO PLAY

The game is played as follows: Shuffle the deck, and then deal five cards to each player. Place the remaining cards facedown on the table. Explain that the object of the game is to collect as many four-card sets (cards with the same name) as possible. The first player asks another player for a name card she or he has (Do you have any cards that say _____?). The player asked must hand over any matching cards. The first player continues asking for name cards until the opponent does not have any that match. The opponent then says, "Go fish," and the first player takes a card from the top of the deck. If the card has the name asked for, the player shows it and gets another turn. If not, the play passes to the player who said, "Go fish." The player with the most sets is the winner.

have prepared a very special version of this game. I am going to show you the names of lots of folks that you know.

◆ Show the 13 names on the cards to the children, spreading them out on the table. (Use the cards with the photos if you have attached them.)

◆ Shuffle the remaining cards and ask the children to sort them, finding three additional matches to the cards spread out. Ask children to read the names aloud as they find them. Read the names for the children if they can't recall them. Call particular attention to the first letter as that will be children's main clue.

> Good guessing, Michael's name does begin with the letter *M*.
>
> Can you hear the /m/ sound in *Michael*?
>
> Can you find the other cards that have the name *Michael* on them?

◆ Teach or remind children how to play the game.

> Remember, your job is to try to get four of each name. I will try to do the same.

◆ Play the game, celebrating the children's ability to match duplicate names as well as to recognize and read names. (Children might be able to match names without being able to read them.) At the beginning, expect to do most of the reading aloud of the names.

> If you forget the name, just show me the card and I will tell you the name you are asking for.

◆ Play until all 13 sets have been matched.

◆ Count the number of sets to determine the winner.

## TIPS TO CONSIDER

◆ If children are reluctant to play this name game, continue to play with a regular deck of cards until they are ready.

◆ Each time you play, review the names on the cards before beginning the game.

◆ Encourage children to read the names on their complete sets at the end of each game.

## POSSIBILITIES TO EXTEND THE LEARNING

• Invite children to help sort the mail that arrives each day, creating a pile for each member of the family. You may want to send some letters to the children so that they can take delight in receiving mail on occasion. Be sure to call their attention to the names printed on the envelopes.

• Search for toys that come with names, pointing the print out to the children. For example, Groovy Girl dolls each have a name printed on the label, as do the trains in the Thomas the Train line.

- Affix "Hello my name is . . ." stickers to large children's dolls and figurines, inviting children to choose names for their toys. (Stickers can be purchased in most office supply stores.) Print names clearly.

- Use parts of familiar names to create and read new words. For example, if Will can read his name, show him how changing the first letter can result in many rhyming words (*bill, dill, fill, gill, hill, mill, pill, quill, sill, chill,* and so on). If Ben can read his name, show him how changing the first letter can result in many rhyming words (*den, hen, Jen, Ken, men, pen, ten, then,* and *when*). Depending on the child's name, you may have to alter some spellings or use parts of names to create rhyming lists of words. For example, Zach may be spelled as Zack or Andie as Andy. Use just the "Wal" in Walter or just the "Fran" in Francine. (Such word-family patterns as *-ill, -ack,* and *-and* are sometimes referred to as "rimes," and they help children generate many, many words.)

- Fill a photo album with pictures of family members and friends. (Snapshots from their birthday parties are especially inviting for young children.) Write names on sticky labels and affix them to or near photos, encouraging children to "read" each label as they turn the pages.

- Using stickers of favorite storybook or pop culture heroes, create a name-matching game. Place several stickers under one another in a column. Print the name of each character mismatched in another column alongside the first. Ask children to draw a line from the sticker to the correct name. Encourage children to use the first letter of the name as a beginning clue.

- Whenever visitors are coming, show children the initials of familiar invited guests. Ask them to guess the name of the visitor based on the initials. Then show children the visitor's full name.

- Label envelopes with names of children's friends, siblings, classmates, and cousins. Cut pictures of toys from toy catalogs, asking children to place each picture in the envelope of the child who would most like that toy. Encourage children to share their choices when they see their friends in person.

- Make children laugh by substituting names of people they know for rhyming words. A few examples follow.

    I am going to write with a <u>Ben</u>. Oops, I mean pen.

    "Let's have some <u>Zach</u>-aroni and cheese for lunch. Oops, I mean macaroni.

    Do you want to put a <u>Kiara</u> on your princess doll? Oops, I mean tiara.

    Uh-oh, a <u>Neil</u> fell off the toy truck. Oops, I mean wheel.

    Please put the flowers on the window <u>Will</u>. Oops, I mean sill.

    Would you like a peanut butter and <u>Shelley</u> sandwich? Oops, I mean jelly.

- Write children's names along with the names of family members or friends in chalk on the sidewalk or playground, creating a long path, with names repeated several times. Ask children to step on their name only, jumping or hopping as they go.

- Point out the names of shops seen frequently in the neighborhood. Children often remember the shop's logo or appearance before they attend to the printed name of the business. For example, young children announce "McDonald's" when they see the arch-shaped *M*. Congratulate children who recognize the name of the neighborhood supermarket, bank, or clothing store. Encourage children to recall the names when you pass by the place of business, spot an advertisement in the daily newspaper, or see passersby with shopping bags from the stores. (See Sign Search on page 109.)

# 35. Clothing Store Shopkeeper

*ACCOMPLISHMENTS: noting environmental print, acquiring sight vocabulary, building concepts*

In this dramatic-play activity, children pretend to sell carefully selected items of clothing, those decorated with words. The game increases children's recognition of words on sight and builds shopping concepts and vocabulary. It is appropriate for children aged 3 to 6.

## MATERIALS TO GATHER

Go through your children's drawers, collecting clothing that is decorated with words. (Schoolchildren can be asked to bring in articles of clothing from home.) Young children's T-shirts, sweatshirts, or pajamas often contain such inspirational words as *peace, love,* or *sweet dreams.* Then, too, children often wear tops that announce their favorite pop-culture heroes, such as Dora, Diego, Bob the Builder, Minnie Mouse, and Harry Potter. Their drawers are also filled with sports words like *baseball, soccer,* and *basketball.* Be sure to include souvenir tops from schools, cities, or neighborhood events. Spread items out on low table or shelf, so that words are easily visible to children.

## INVITATIONS TO PLAY

◆ Introduce the activity, pointing to and reading aloud the words to children.

   Would you like to pretend to go clothes shopping today?

   First let's look at all the items that we have for sale. This one says "Hope," and that one says "Blast Off."

◆ Read all the words to children and then reread them, encouraging children to recall the words.

◆ Invite children to play shopkeeper.

   Now we are ready to play. You can be the shopkeeper, and I will be the customer.

◆ Challenge the shopkeeper to find specific items.

   I am looking for a size 3T, long-sleeved green shirt that says "Love" in shiny pink sequins.

   Do you have any green cotton pajamas for boys in size 2T that says "Zoo Keeper" on them?

   Do you have a hooded red sweatshirt in size 4T that says "Columbia University" on it?

◆ Continue until all the items are purchased.

## TIPS TO CONSIDER

◆ Be sure to describe each item in detail to expand the children's vocabulary. However if you sense that children are selecting the item based on the other descriptors rather than the words, limit your descriptions. For example, simply say, "I am looking for a shirt with the word *baseball* on it."

◆ Children may decide to play with the clothing. Let them, asking, "What does your shirt say?"

◆ Children may expect money during the exchange. Use play money, draw pretend coins and dollars, or use real coins, depending on the age of the children.

◆ Children may want to reverse roles, choosing to be the shopper. If so, encourage them to ask for particular articles.

## POSSIBILITIES TO EXTEND THE LEARNING

• Engage children in shopping conversations by including such questions and comments as the following:

How much does it cost?

Do you take credit cards?

Here's your money.

Do I get any change?

• Get in the habit of sending children on "word" errands.

Please bring me your brother's pajamas, the ones that say "night-night" on them.

Please put your "Little Friends Camp" T-shirt into the hamper.

Your "Columbia University" sweatshirt just fell off the hook. Please hang it up.

• Once children can read all the words on their items of clothing, teach them to read the words on the sweatshirts, T-shirts, and aprons you frequently wear.

• When shopping for new clothes in a department store, be sure to read aloud any words printed on the clothing to the children, allowing them some choice—for example, "Do you want the shirt that says 'New York Yankees' or the one that says 'New York Mets'?"

Look Who's Learning to Read

# 36. Household Rubbings

*ACCOMPLISHMENTS: learning sight vocabulary*

It's not hard to impress children aged 2 to 6. In this activity, children watch in awe as you make words appear everywhere. In actuality, you have placed a sheet of paper over an object that has raised or etched letters. As you glide a crayon across the entire surface, the word "magically" appears. Children learn words by sight when they do frequent rubbings of them. With support, even 2½-year-olds can produce a rubbing. Older children can do these on their own.

## MATERIALS TO GATHER

Search your home, apartment, or classroom for objects with raised or etched print. Possibilities include refrigerator magnets, credit cards, keys, plastic containers with etched logos, metal mailboxes with the words U.S. Mail, toys with brand names imprinted on lids, shoe soles, coins, wooden alphabet blocks, paperweights, license plates, and brand names on household appliances. Also gather some plain white paper and crayons.

## INVITATIONS TO PLAY

◆ If children have never done a rubbing, you might begin with any surface with an interesting texture, rather than only those with raised or etched letters.

 Remember when we did rubbings of these ceramic tiles, these carved serving platters, and the faces of these coins?

 Today we are going to do rubbings on things that have words on them. And we are going to watch the words appear as we rub our crayons up and down over these surfaces. I will do a few to show you how it's done.

◆ Demonstrate how to make a rubbing of a few of the items gathered.

 Rub up and down so that whole letters are complete before you move to the next letter.

◆ Show the rubbing alongside the original when complete, asking children to check if all the letters appeared. Read the words to the children twice, once from the original and a second time from the rubbing.

◆ Invite children to pick items for rubbing. Support their efforts by holding the object steady or guiding their hand with the crayon if necessary.

◆ Display children's rubbings on the wall.

## TIPS TO CONSIDER

◆ If children are not ready to recall whole words, use the rubbings as an opportunity to review the letters of the alphabet.

 Here comes a *U*. Now I see an *S*. Now you've made an *M*.

 Here comes the *A*. Keep going. Now I see part of the *I*.

Okay, here's the last letter. It's an *L*.

◆ If children are ready, have them call out the letters.

◆ Children may want to do rubbings across the page (horizontally), so that no one letter is complete until the entire surface has been rubbed. If that is the case, postpone calling out letters until they are complete.

◆ Children may not be able to press down hard enough to make a successful rubbing. Use dark-colored crayons and be ready to help children make the rubbings.

You rub first and I'll put another layer on top of yours.

◆ You may not want to use coins as the print may be too small for young children to read the letters or the words.

## POSSIBILITIES TO EXTEND THE LEARNING

• Every once in while, refer back to the gallery of completed rubbings, asking children if they recall the words. Remind children if they have forgotten.

• Keep your eye out for other objects for potential rubbings. Ask children to do the same.

• Some objects, like the mailbox, are found out of doors. Do an outdoor rubbing search with children. Make sure you have chosen safe surfaces to work on.

# 37. Sign Search

*ACCOMPLISHMENTS: understanding the meaning and value of signs, building sight vocabulary*

Neighborhood walks are filled with opportunities to note environmental print (words that appear naturally and frequently in familiar settings). In this activity, children are asked to pay attention to signs, understanding their meaning and value. This neighborhood stroll also helps to expand children's vocabulary, increase their attention span, develop new concepts, and engage in interesting conversations. This activity is appropriate for all youngsters, particularly those who show an interest in print.

## MATERIALS TO GATHER

This activity requires no preparation other than a willingness to take a slow neighborhood walk. Large index cards and markers will come in handy to record the signs spotted when you return home or back to school.

## INVITATIONS TO PLAY

◆ On any neighborhood stroll, be prepared to do a lot of stopping, pointing out, and explaining.

Do you see that red sign over there on the corner, the one with a hexagon shape? You have to look way up on that pole to see it. I think we have that same sign on our train set. Do you know what it says?

It says Stop. *S-T-O-P*. Those letters spell *stop*. All the cars, trucks, taxis, and buses have to stop when they see that sign on the corner.

Why do you think we need that sign?

◆ Respond to children's comments and answer any questions that the children ask.

Let's keep walking and see if we see any other Stop signs.

◆ Point out any additional Stop signs, encouraging children to discover them on their own.

There are lots of other signs to help drivers and the people on the street stay safe. Look at that black-and-white one up there. Do you see there is an arrow pointing in one direction? (Point with your hand to reinforce meaning.) That sign says One Way. Do you know how that sign helps drivers and people walking across the street?

Let's find a few more One Way signs.

◆ Continue pointing out other neighborhood signs. These might include Caution, Detour, Please Curb Your Dog, and Keep Off the Grass, as well as street names. Be sure to explain what all the signs mean and why they are helpful.

◆ Be sure to point out signs in store windows as well. These might include Open, Closed, Exit, Come In We're Open, and Welcome. Include the name of any neighborhood supermarket, especially if children are likely to spot people carrying shopping bags adorned with the store name and logo. (Then too, when studying shop windows, take the opportunity to explain the names of different workers. Don't hesitate to include such "sophisticated" words as *manicurist, seamstress, florist,* and *jeweler.*)

◆ You can also point out the signs on trucks that are frequently seen in your neighborhood. These might include UPS, FedEx, and U.S. Mail.

◆ When you return home, record the signs that you spotted.

Let's try to remember the signs we saw today. I'll write them down so we can look them over every once in a while.

◆ Write each one on a separate index card. Add visual clues to help children recall the words. For example, draw grass on the card that reads Keep Off the Grass. Encourage children to watch or help you as you prepare each card.

## TIPS TO CONSIDER

◆ Be prepared to lift young children out of their strollers to make signs more visible.

◆ Don't expect children to remember any or all of the signs when you first begin pointing them out. This activity can be repeated on any outing.

◆ Be sure to congratulate children the first time they remember a word on sight.

◆ Celebrate the occasion when children ask, "What does that sign say?"

Good for you for asking! That sign says _____.

## POSSIBILITIES TO EXTEND THE LEARNING

• On your next neighborhood outing, take along the stack of index cards on which you recorded the names of signs you've spotted. Ask children to match the cards to real signs.

• Borrow and share picture books from the public library that highlight street and road signs. Take a walk with the book in hand, looking for the signs depicted. Suggested titles include the following:

*City Signs* by Zoran Milich
*I See a Sign* by Lars Klove
*Mr. Pine's Mixed-Up Signs* by Leonard Kessler
*Once Upon a Banana* by Jennifer Armstrong
*Red, Yellow, Green: What Do Signs Mean?* by Joan Holub
*The Signmaker's Assistant* by Tedd Arnold

• Help children to make paper or cardboard signs for their block constructions and their dramatic play.

• Photograph or draw neighborhood signs. Then help children create their own books of signs.

*Look Who's Learning to Read*

# 38. Map Brochure Memory Game

*ACCOMPLISHMENTS: increasing visual memory, acquiring sight vocabulary*

This activity extends and enriches visits to parks, museums, or zoos by asking children to recall what they learned on those outings. The game also helps young children build memory skills and older children develop sight vocabulary. It is appropriate for children aged 2½ and up.

## MATERIALS TO GATHER

Whenever visiting a museum, an amusement park, a botanical garden, or a zoo, pick up two copies of the free map or guide brochure. (Most places are happy to give one to each child as well as one to the adult.) Upon returning home, be sure to show children a whole brochure before cutting up the two copies for this activity.

Look over the brochure, searching for small labeled photographs, preferably of things you noted on your visit. Be sure to cut photos to approximately the same size. (If the photos aren't labeled, you can write them yourself.) Cut duplicate photos, one from each brochure.

Glue photos onto small cardboard rectangles. (Five sets of duplicate photos would enable you to play Concentration, the classic memory game.) All cardboard shapes should be the same size. Cut cardboard to fit the size of your photos.

Here, duplicate copies of the map from the Bronx Zoo in New York City are used. All the key signposts were clipped and mounted on small cardboard rectangles. Photos from the Monkey House, the World of Birds, Sea Lions, Baboons, Birds of Prey, Himalayan Highlands, Jungle World, Bears, the World of Reptiles, and Giraffes were clearly labeled. These ten sets of photos were glued onto 20 cardboard cutouts (approximately 2 inches by 2½ inches). Cardboard was cut from the back of yellow steno pads.

## INVITATIONS TO PLAY

◆ Introduce the game.

Right here in this envelope are all the pieces I made for a new game.

Do you remember our visit last week to the zoo? And do you remember the brochure that the zoo worker gave us so that we could find our way easily around the zoo? I have used that brochure to make a game for us to play.

Let's look at all these cards. I have made two of each one.

◆ Review all the cards, naming each sight and recalling events from your visit. Then explain how to play the game.

Now I am going to turn the cards facedown, mix them up, and place them on the table in neat rows.

You get to pick two cards. If they match, you can hold onto the cards and pick two more. If they don't match, you have to place them facedown in the same spot on the table. Then it will be my turn.

◆ Continue alternating turns until all the cards are gone. The player with the most sets is the winner.

## TIPS TO CONSIDER

◆ Be sure to refer to the brochure during your visit. Point out the actual places in the park, museum, garden, or zoo that will become part of your game at home.

◆ Encourage children to try and remember a returned card's spot on the table.
  Okay, I am turning over that giraffe card right here. You may need that card soon.

◆ Keep the card sets in a labeled envelope for reuse.

◆ Play the game before making a return visit.

## POSSIBILITIES TO EXTEND THE LEARNING

• With very young children, you can play a simple matching game with the cards—just arrange them faceup on the table and have children find the pairs.

• Ask older children to read the labels when they make a match.

• Share any interesting fact you know about the object of the photo each time you make a match. For example, when matching the giraffe photos, you could add, "Did you know that male giraffes have thicker horns than female giraffes?" Encourage children to share what they know as well.

• Ask questions each time you make a match. For example, when matching baboons, you could ask, "What kinds of fruits do you think baboons like to eat?" Try to research answers to your questions on the next visit to the site or on a visit to the library.

• As a variation, prepare a Kitchen Counter Concentration game. Save empty cartons from children's favorite cereals, cookies, and snacks. Clip same-size squares around product logos, two matching ones for each product. Turn cardboard squares over to the blank sides and play a Concentration game with older children or leave them face-up to play a matching game with younger children.

Look Who's Learning to Read

# 39. Outdoor Bingo

*ACCOMPLISHMENTS: paying attention to environment, learning new vocabulary and concepts, developing sight vocabulary*

In this outdoor activity, children are asked to pay careful attention to their environment. The game can be played when you are pushing a stroller around the neighborhood or taking a group of youngsters on a neighborhood walk. The activity teaches concepts, expands vocabulary, heightens attention to the environment, and encourages word recognition for older children. It is appropriate for children aged 2½ and up.

## MATERIALS TO GATHER

Cut cardboard rectangles from old gift boxes or large cereal boxes and use the blank sides to create Bingo boards. You can also use old manila folders. The important thing is that the material is heavy enough to allow children to hold it stiff and that the squares are large enough for you to draw on them the board shown below. Any pieces of cardboard approximately 9 inches wide and 12 inches long will do.

Collect an assortment of stickers. Any will do, including those given out as party favors, purchased, or sent in the mail as part of advertisements.

Using a dark-colored marker, divide the cardboard into 12 boxes by drawing a three-by-four grid. Boxes should be approximately 2¼ inches wide and 4 inches long. (See example at right.)

Using a pen, draw and label a familiar item in each box, one that can be seen on a stroll in your neighborhood or school community. Items might include a fire hydrant, a mailbox, a police car, a bicycle, a squirrel, a bird, a dog, a cat, a fire engine, a stop sign, a taxi, a flower, a gate, a cloud, a motorcycle, a bus, a ladder, a flag, a balloon, a One Way sign, and an ice-cream cone.

Leave an outlined space in which a sticker can be placed when children spot the item. Make as many boards as needed for the children in your care.

Each time you create a new board, be sure to rearrange the order of the items and substitute a few new and interesting ones. For example, you might add an awning, a scaffold, a fire escape, or an evergreen tree.

## INVITATIONS TO PLAY

◆ Introduce this new version of Bingo.

Would you like to play a very special game when we take our morning walk today?

Look at these cards I made especially for you. Do you know what all these things are?

◆ Review the names of the items.

When we are walking today, we are going to try and spot each of these things.

Each time you find one, I am going to give you a little sticker to place in the box. The stickers will help us keep a record of the things we have seen.

◆ Explain how the game ends.

If you do find all of the items on the card, and the whole board is covered with stickers, you can call out "Bingo!"

## TIPS TO CONSIDER

◆ Simple drawings work best. But if you feel inadequate as an artist, you can cut some items out of magazines or copy pictures of items from children's books or puzzles.

◆ Be sure to go over the names of each item before leaving the house, apartment, or school.

◆ Be the gatekeeper of the stickers, handing them out when items are spotted.

◆ Children may stare at the card instead of at neighborhood scenes. Remind them to keep looking around. Spot some yourself to demonstrate.

◆ Encourage children to place stickers in the designated spaces, not covering the drawing or label. (If drawings and words are visible, there is more of a likelihood that older children will begin to recognize words.)

◆ Younger children may not be able to place sticker down in just the right space. Be patient and offer assistance.

◆ If some items aren't spotted, the game can be continued on another day.

◆ As an alternate way to play, children can call out "Bingo!" when they've covered one row with stickers, rather than the entire card.

## POSSIBILITIES TO EXTEND THE LEARNING

• Board items can be connected to a theme. For example, 12 community workers (police officer, mail carrier, firefighter, taxi driver, doorman, delivery person, crossing guard, ice cream vendor, greengrocer, florist, ambulance driver, baker), 12 kinds of vehicles, or 12 kinds of plants.

• If you are caring for two children in a double stroller, each can have his or her own card. There are no winners or losers, as you keep walking until both cards are completed. Older children can have more specific items on their cards. For example, younger children can look for a bird, older ones for a pigeon.

• Create the board together with the children.

Let's make a board together. What items do you think we should include?

Look Who's Learning to Read

# 40. Old Calendars/New Fun

*ACCOMPLISHMENTS: recognizing words on sight, following directions,
learning vocabulary and concepts connected to themes*

This game offers an easy and inexpensive way to introduce youngsters to board games, and it's designed to meet the needs and interests of the children in your care. Children follow calendar spaces around until they reach the last day of the month, the box with the big "payoff." In addition to creating the theme of the game and the specialty spaces along the way (both lucky and unlucky ones), children receive practice in counting and begin to recognize words on sight. Appropriate for children aged 3 and up.

## MATERIALS TO GATHER

Save your old calendars, particularly ones that have large boxes and have not been written upon. A calendar page, a numbered spinner or die from an old game, and different-colored buttons are all you need for this homemade game. (See example at right.)

## INVITATIONS TO PLAY

◆ Introduce the materials.

Today, I am going to show you how to make our very own game. We're going to turn this calendar page into a game board.

| S | M | T | W | T | F | S |
|---|---|---|---|---|---|---|
| | | | 1 START | 2 | 3 | 4 EGG ③ |
| 5 | 6 | 7 ② SPRINKLES | 8 | 9 | 10 ③ BURNT | 11 |
| 12 | 13 | 14 ② HEART | 15 | 16 ② FRIEND | 17 | 18 |
| 19 | 20 ③ NO SUGAR | 21 | 22 | 23 | 24 | 25 |
| 26 | 27 | 28 | 29 | 30 | 31 END!!! | |

THE BAKING COOKIES GAME

◆ Demonstrate how to leapfrog (jump) from the last box on one row to the first box on the next row. In other words, you're going to follow the spaces in numerical order from 1 straight through to 28, 29, 30, or 31.

We are going to start right here at number 1 and travel through all the numbers until we get to the end. In this month, January, there are 31 days for us to pass through.

◆ Explain and demonstrate the use of the die.

We toss the die, and whatever number lands on top is the number of spaces we have to move.

◆ Decide on the theme of the game, giving a few examples.

Now we have to decide what our game will be about. We have to choose something that we really want to happen so that we will be so happy to get to the last box and be winners.

Would you like to make a game about baking chocolate chip cookies? Or one about having a birthday party or learning to ride a bicycle or learning how to swim? Or maybe we could make one about going trick-or-treating, visiting your cousin's house, or flying to the moon!

◆ Encourage children to select one of the topics suggested, or come up with an original one.

> Baking cookies? That's sounds like fun.

◆ Design the game board.

> I am going to write the word *start* in the first box and the word *end* in the last box. Would you like to draw a cookie in this last box? Would you like to add chips to the cookie?

> Now let's think of three really happy things that could happen while we bake cookies and then three unhappy things that could happen.

◆ As children come up with ideas enter them on random boxes around the board (calendar page).

◆ If a player lands on a happy space, she goes ahead two boxes (you can choose any number of spaces). If she lands on an unhappy space, she goes back three boxes (you can choose any number of spaces).

◆ Add picture clues to help children recall the words.

◆ A number of possibilities follow:

> Hurray, we added sprinkles to the cookies—go ahead two boxes. So let's draw a cookie with sprinkles in this space. Then I'll write the word *sprinkles* and the number 2.

> Hurray, we used heart-shaped cookie cutters—go ahead two boxes. So let's draw a heart in this space over here. Then I'll write the word *heart* and the number 2.

> Hurray, we shared our cookies with a friend—go ahead two boxes. Let's draw some friends sharing a cookie. Where shall we put it? Then I will write the word *friend* and the number 2.

> Now let's do the unhappy ones.

> Uh-oh, we dropped eggs on the floor—go back three spaces. Let's draw a cracked egg dripping onto the floor. Which space shall we fill? Then I will write the word *egg* and the number 3.

> Uh-oh, we ran out of sugar—go back three spaces. Let's draw a spoonful of sugar. Where would you like to put it? Then I will write the word *sugar* and the number 3.

> Uh-oh, we burned the first batch—go back three spaces. Let's draw a burnt cookie. Where do you think this one should go? Then I will write the word *burnt* and the number 3.

◆ Choose different-colored buttons as markers and play, taking turns throwing the die and moving the designated number of spaces.

## TIPS TO CONSIDER

◆ Remove page from bound calendar so it can lie flat on a tabletop.

◆ You could add a happy face or a sad face to remind children if they have landed on something good or bad.

◆ You could add arrows to remind players if they go backward or forward when they land on any of the six specialty spaces.

◆ Be sure to spread the specialty spaces around the board.

◆ Let children do as much of the drawing as possible.

◆ Some children might need help counting spaces and moving around the board.

◆ You might prefer not to leapfrog back to the beginning of each week, instead alternating traveling left to right, dropping down a row, traveling right to left, dropping down again, then traveling left to right, and so on. If you do so, you may want to cross off the numbers and add guiding arrows to remind players of the direction to follow.

◆ To avoid having winners and losers, you can continue the play until all players reach the cookies.

◆ Save game pieces in an envelope to play again on another day.

## POSSIBILITIES TO EXTEND THE LEARNING

• Make more homemade board games from other calendar pages. As children mature, encourage them to offer more of the ideas for the games and to do more of the drawing and eventually the writing.

• Introduce the use of current calendars. Hang them in children's rooms to teach the names of the months and the days of the week (and their abbreviations), as well as the names of any holidays that are printed on the calendar. Gradually use the calendar to help children remember upcoming appointments, special events, play dates, and so on. Children will learn a great deal by watching you mark the calendar. Teach children who are interested how to mark off days on the calendar and do countdowns to special days.

# 41. Food Festivities

*ACCOMPLISHMENTS: learning sight words, engaging in dramatic play, writing words*

Whether children are voracious eaters or fussy ones, the topic of food is a popular one with parents and children alike. In this activity, children have an opportunity to think about which foods they would prefer at different mealtimes as well as for snacks. Along the way, they begin to recognize food names on sight, have opportunities to sort foods, and are inspired to use food clippings and labels in their dramatic play. This activity is appropriate for children aged 3 and up.

## MATERIALS TO GATHER

To carry out this activity, you will need to gather parenting or family magazines, index cards, dark markers, and glue or tape. Clip pictures of familiar foods from the magazines. Then mount and label them on small index cards. Be sure to gather foods that would be appropriate for breakfast, lunch, and dinner as well as healthy snacks. Label four envelopes with the words "Breakfast," "Lunch," "Dinner," and "Snacks." Materials can be gathered with children or prepared in advance. Additional paper and markers will be needed to play the game.

## INVITATIONS TO PLAY

◆ If cards have been prepared, share them with the children, inviting them to sort the cards into labeled envelopes. If pictures are to be clipped, labeled, and mounted with children, browse magazines together, cutting out pictures of a wide range of familiar foods.

Last night I read some of my magazines, and when I finished reading them, I decided to clip pictures of foods that you enjoy.

◆ Show the cards to children, reading the names of the foods and/or the brand names if they are familiar ones.

Here are four envelopes, one each for breakfast, lunch, dinner, and snacks. Would you help me sort this stack of cards, putting the foods into the envelope that makes the most sense? You'll have to decide which envelope is the best match.

Where do you think eggs belong?

How about apples?

When do you think you should eat corn?

◆ When all the foods are sorted, use the cards for dramatic play, if children's energy is high.

How about playing "Restaurant" with these cards?

We can use the words on the cards to make up a menu.

◆ If children are able to write, invite them to copy the names of the foods onto a piece of paper labeled "Menu." If they are not ready to write on their own, copy the food names from each envelope, creating a menu for each meal.

◆ Decide on roles. Be sure to switch roles at some point.

   Do you want to be the waiter (or waitress) or the hungry customer?

◆ If children are waiters, offer pads and pencils for taking orders. Encourage the use of invented spelling for beginning writers or pretend writing for those not ready to make any sound-symbol correspondences. (Children who can't yet write often make a series of mountain peaks or loops to represent writing or put down random strings of letters just to show they understand the meaning of writing. See pages 127–129 for more information on beginning writing.)

◆ Encourage children to sift through the envelopes searching for the foods that were ordered.

   The pictures and the words can help you find the foods I ordered.

◆ If children are hungry customers, help them read the menu, as no pictures appear there. Show the children the words you write as you take their orders. Say the words slowly, writing the letters as you make the sounds associated with the letters. In other words, stretch out the word so that the children can hear all the sounds. The word *milk* would be said slowly enough to hear all these sounds: /m/-/i/-/l/-/k/.

## TIPS TO CONSIDER

◆ Choose magazines that are likely to have abundant advertisements of familiar as well as healthy foods. If magazine clippings contain food packaging with a prominent label, there is no need to rewrite the name of the product. In other words, if the photo of the packaged food contains the words "Fig Newtons," there is no need to rewrite the name by hand. Children learn a great deal by recognizing the labels they see on their kitchen counters.

◆ As you browse, clip, and sort, encourage conversation about nutrition, favorite foods, cooking, and mealtimes.

◆ Many foods can be eaten at several mealtimes, so be prepared to accept children's choices.

## POSSIBILITIES TO EXTEND THE LEARNING

• Cut illustrations and labels from supermarket fliers and mount them on cards. Ask children to help you find the matching products as you travel the aisles.

• Take a leisurely tour of the fruit section of a supermarket, inviting children to name each fruit, touch its surface, describe its shape and color, sniff for aroma, and "read" its label. Buy a few to make fruit salad.

• When cooking or baking, print the names of the ingredients on separate index cards. Encourage children to locate what's needed by matching the word on the card to the label on the container or bag of baking powder, flour, sugar, baking soda, or other ingredient.

Now I need to scoop out a cup of flour. This card says "flour." Which bag has the word *flour* on it?

- After baking is done, see if children can recall any of the words on the cards.

- Collect takeout menus from local restaurants. Make a list of children's favorite foods. Read the list aloud to children, providing simple picture clues to help children recall the items. Ask children to locate and circle or highlight their favorite foods on the takeout menus.

- Share picture books that include recipes for young readers and beginning chefs. A few possibilities follow:

  *Apple Farmer Annie* by Monica Wellington

  *Bee-Bim Bop* by Linda Sue Park

  *The Bye-Bye Pie* by Sharon Jennings

  *A Cake All for Me!* by Karen Magnuson Beil

  *Carrot Soup* by John Segal

  *Cook-a-Doodle-Doo!* by Janet Stevens and Susan Stevens Crummel

  *The Cookie-Store Cat* by Cynthia Rylant

  *A Day With My Aunts/Un día con mis tías* Anilú Bernardo

  *Jingle Dancer* by Cynthia Leitich Smith

  *The Moon Might Be Milk* by Lisa Shulman

  *Mr. Cookie Baker* by Monica Wellington

  *Pizza at Sally's* by Monica Wellington

# LANGUAGE PLAY

## 42. Language Delights

*ACCOMPLISHMENTS: appreciating and creating metaphors, listening to read-alouds*

Many of the activities described in this book involve playing with language. These include all the rhyming activities as well as Silly Sandwich Syllable Strings (page 95), Songs With a Twist (page 79), and Old Songs, New Versions (page 86). In this activity, children are immersed in the use of metaphors, one way writers make comparisons. Children are asked to use such literary language to say kind things about their friends, family members, and even themselves. This activity is appropriate for children aged 3½ and up.

## MATERIALS TO GATHER

Kathi Appelt's picture book *Incredible Me!* is a perfect way to introduce how writers use language in clever ways to help convey their meaning. If this book is not available, the same concept can be introduced without it, as described below.

## INVITATIONS TO PLAY

◆ Share and discuss *Incredible Me!*

◆ Reread, highlighting the main character's comments that begin with the words "I'm the . . ." Probe children's understandings of such metaphorical language.

　Why do you think the young girl announces that she is the cream in the butter, the salt in the sea, the dill in the pickle, the beat in the jazz, and so on?

◆ Explain any unknown terms to children. Help them understand that the way the little girl talks about herself lets us know that she is very proud of herself.

　If you are the cream in the butter, or the dill in the pickle, or the beat in the jazz, you are very important. Jazz wouldn't be jazz without the beat, pickles wouldn't taste like pickles without dill, and butter wouldn't be butter if you didn't begin with cream.

◆ Explain how using words and ideas like these is a very fine way to make someone feel good.

　The little girl in the story was talking about herself, but she could also talk that way about her friends to make them feel important. If I said those kind things about you, you would feel very special.

◆ If *Incredible Me!* is not available, a similar use of metaphors can be introduced as follows:

　How would you feel if I told you, "You are the frosting on my cupcake"? What if I said, "You are the basketball in my hoop!"? What do you think I mean when I say, "You are the bubbles in my bathtub"?

Explain to children how these expressions all suggest wonderful things.

Of course I don't mean that you are really frosting or a basketball or bubbles. I mean you are something important, wonderful, and special! Those are compliments.

◆ Introduce a very simple "parlor" game.

What if I wanted to say something so nice to you and I began,

"You are the rose in my . . ." What would make sense to say there?

◆ Be accepting of any answer that makes sense.

Yes, "You are the rose in my garden" is quite a compliment. "You are the rose in my bouquet" would be a lovely thing to say as well.

◆ Continue playing with language, asking children to fill in these other kind thoughts.

You are the stars in my _____ (sky).

You are the float in my _____ (parade).

You are the candles on my _____ (birthday cake).

You are the locomotive on my _____ (train).

You are the sand on my _____ (beach).

You are the peak on my _____ (mountain).

You are the apple in my_____ (pie).

You are the salt on my _____ (pretzel).

◆ Invite children to invent their own compliments by beginning with the words "You are the . . ."?

Can you think of something kind to say to me, beginning with the words, "You're the . . ."?

◆ Be appreciative of children's offerings.

◆ Suggest ways to get really good at offering these kinds of compliments.

Whenever someone does something kind, we can all say something very special to them, beginning with the words "You are the . . ."

When we give and get bedtime hugs and kisses, we can all say good-night in this very special way.

## TIPS TO CONSIDER

◆ Follow the read-aloud tips on pages 10–12.

◆ Whenever you discover clever uses of language or language play, share these with gusto.

◆ Encourage children to ask questions about language and take time to answer them.

## POSSIBILITIES TO EXTEND THE LEARNING

- Help children record their special ways of giving compliments and then turn these into thank-you notes and greeting cards for birthdays and holidays.

- Share and discuss metaphors in Maryann K. Cusimano's *You Are My I Love You* and Rebecca Doughty's *You Are to Me*.

- Share and discuss Susan Creech's picture book *Fishing in the Air*. Upon rereading the book, note the author's use of similes, comparisons containing the words *as* or *like*. Also share *I Love You as Much . . .* by Laura Krauss Melmed and Norton Juster's *As Silly as Knees, As Busy as Bees: An Astounding Assortment of Similes*. Explain any unfamiliar comparisons.

- Engage children in other forms of language play by sharing the following picture books:

    *31 Uses for a Mom* by Harriet Ziefert

    *40 Uses for a Grandpa* by Harriet Ziefert

    *Amelia Bedelia* by Peggy Parrish

    *Busy Buzzing Bumblebees and Other Tongue Twisters* by Alvin Schwartz

    *A Chocolate Moose for Dinner* by Fred Gwynne

    *Cook-a-Doodle-Doo!* by Janet Stevens and Susan Stevens Crummel

    *Did You Say Pears?* by Arlene Alda

    *Don't Forget the Bacon* by Pat Hutchins

    *Henry! The Dog With No Tail* by Kate Feiffer

    *Hey, Hay! A Wagonful of Funny Homonym Riddles* by Marvin Terban

    *A Honey of a Day* by Janet Marshall

    *A Huge Hog Is a Big Pig: A Rhyming Word Game* by Francis McCall and Patricia Keeler

    *The King Who Rained* by Fred Gwynne

    *Knock, Knock!* by Saxton Freymann

    *A Little Pigeon Toad* by Fred Gwynne

    *My Teacher Likes to Say* by Denise Brennan-Nelson

    *Orange Pear Apple Bear* by Emily Gravett

    *Tongue Twisters to Tangle Your Tongue* by Rebecca Cobb

- Play a question-and-answer game with some specially chosen words. Try answering questions with such words as *actually*, *of course*, *but*, or *although*. For example, if you agree to play with the word *but*, the children ask you questions and you must weave the word *but* into your answers. The children might ask, "What's your favorite color?" And you might answer, "I like green, *but* I really love brown." Children ask, "What are we eating for lunch?" You answer, "Maybe we'll have scrambled eggs, *but* I am really in the mood for grilled cheese." Reverse roles, with you asking the questions and children attempting to insert the chosen words into their answers.

# 43. Poetry Play

*ACCOMPLISHMENTS: appreciating rhythm and rhyme, learning new vocabulary, learning poems by heart, appreciating sounds of language and strong images*

Poetry enriches children's lives in many ways. They hear lullabies as infants in their cribs, finger plays in their high chairs, and jump-rope rhymes in the playground, and, if they are very lucky, they listen to a grown-up read beautiful poetry from carefully selected anthologies at bedtime. In this activity, children get to know one poetry anthology really well. They learn poems by heart, appreciate rhythm and rhyme, learn new vocabulary, appreciate the sounds of words as well as strong images, and hopefully develop a lifelong appreciation of poetry. This activity is appropriate for children of all ages.

## MATERIALS TO GATHER

All this activity requires is one poetry collection or anthology. Be sure to choose one that will appeal to you and the children in your care, as you will spend a great deal of time with it. Make sure the content of the poems is appropriate for the ages and interests of your children, and be sure any illustrations enhance the meaning of the poems. Very young children take easily to rhyming poems, but not all poems in an anthology need to rhyme to satisfy young listeners. Then, too, not all poems need to be funny to capture the hearts of young children. Expect children to experience a wide range of emotions, including sympathy, happiness, and even fear. Most of all, choose poems that have satisfying and/or comforting endings. You can choose a collection of poems written by one poet or an edited anthology representing many poets. See Must-Know Poets in the Appendix (page 156).

Here, the collection *I Never Did That Before* by Lilian Moore is shared.

## INVITATIONS TO PLAY

◆ Introduce the collection, inviting children to talk about the title and cover illustrations. (There is no need to define poetry for young children. Trust the poets to convey this very special way of sharing ideas.)

I have picked a very special book to share with you today. It's called *I Never Did That Before*. Lilian Moore wrote the words, and another Lillian, Lillian Hoban, made the illustrations. Look at the children on the cover. Why do you think each of them might be saying, "I never did that before"?

Have you ever said, "I never did that before"?

◆ Invite children to recall things they tried doing for the very first time.

That's right—remember the first time you tasted sushi and the first time you tried to throw a bowling ball. You might have said, "Wow, I never did that before!"

Lilian Moore is a very special kind of writer. She is called a poet. And this book is filled with her poems. This book has 14 of her poems. And here on this very first page is a list of the titles of her poems. I'll read them to you and you can tell me which poem you'd like to hear first.

◆ Show the table of contents, explaining how useful this page is. Read the list of titles if the collection is not too large.

◆ If the title of the collection is particularly meaningful, as it is here, demonstrate how the title of the collection and the title of the poem help you imagine what the poem will be about.

> You chose the poem "Monkey Bars," and now we know that we can find it on page 6. Remember, this collection is called *I Never Did That Before*, so I'm guessing that the poem is about a child who went on the monkey bars for the very first time. Let's see if I'm right.

◆ Let children study and talk about the illustrations.

◆ Read the poem at least twice before discussing it.

◆ Invite comments and questions, as well as any stories the children have to tell in response to the poem.

◆ Continue sharing other poems in the collection in the same way.

## TIPS TO CONSIDER

◆ It helps to read poems to yourself before reading them aloud to children. Rehearsing can help you read the poems in a meaningful way, honoring their rhyme, rhythm, and repetition.

◆ Be sure to pause briefly at the end of each line even if the thought does not as yet sound complete. The poet writes the poem in the manner she wants it read.

◆ Make endings sound like endings. You might consider saying the words slower, louder, or softer, depending on the meaning that you think the poet is conveying.

### POSSIBILITIES TO EXTEND THE LEARNING

• Reread the collection aloud as often as possible.

• When rhyming poems become familiar, try leaving off the last word in a rhyme for children to fill in.

• Attempt to memorize an entire poem, inviting children to do so as well. Select an easy one for young children, and if children are enthusiastic, help them recite the poem for visitors.

• Copy favorite poems on large sheets of paper, taking care to copy the words exactly as they appear in the book. Print words neatly and boldly, and hang in children's bedrooms. Read the poems aloud as part of your bedtime ritual. (In classrooms, favorite poems can become part of end-of-day rituals.) During the day, ask children who are ready to spot high-interest words.

> Can you find the words *monkey bars* two times on this paper?

• If children are unable to spot the words, show them the first place they appear and ask them to find the second place.

• Refer to poetry collections, individual poems, or memorable lines from poems in everyday activities. For example, children can be encouraged to say, "I never did that before," whenever they try something new.

- Learn by heart and recite poems that relate to children's favorite activities. Try reciting Dorothy Aldis's poem "Hiding" whenever you play hide-and-seek or the first verse of Christopher Morley's poem "Animal Crackers" whenever you offer snacks. (Ask a librarian to help locate more poems in poetry anthologies.)

- Be supportive when poems inspire dramatic play and artwork.

    Are those dolls at the playground? Is this one going on the monkey bars for the very first time? That's just great. We know how she must feel.

    Are you drawing an upside-down boy hanging on the monkey bars? That's a great challenge, good for you!

- Copy children's favorite poems and have children illustrate them to give as gifts.

- Help children discover favorite poets. If there is a poem the children love in an edited anthology, look for additional works by its author. If you have shared a collection of works by one poet, look for other collections by the same poet.

- Periodically, borrow additional poetry anthologies from the public library and let children acquire new tastes in poetry. Ask librarians to recommend collections of riddle poems, shape poems, free-verse poems, haiku, and other types of poems. Borrow collections based on a theme of interest to your children as well as single poems presented in picture-book format.

- Select poetry collections or individual poems that lend themselves to special events or experiences. A few examples follow:
    - Jump rope with rhymes from *Over in the Pink House: New Jump Rope Rhymes* by Rebecca Kai Dotlich.
    - Refer to a map of the United States as you share poems from *In Aunt Giraffe's Green Garden* by Jack Prelutsky.
    - When children welcome a new baby into the family, share *B Is for Baby: An Alphabet of Verses* by Myra Cohn Livingston.
    - Make the reading of Sylvia Plath's *The Bed Book*, a poem published in picture book format, part of bedtime rituals.
    - Recite Robert Louis Stevenson's *Block City*, another poem published in picture book format, whenever children make block constructions.

# BEGINNING WRITING

## 44. Name Ten Sheets

*ACCOMPLISHMENTS: using invented spelling, expanding vocabulary and concepts*

Children love challenges, especially ones that make them feel as if they are becoming more grown-up. In this simple activity, children are asked to think of ten things that belong in the same category. The activity can be done orally, but it takes on new dimensions when children attempt to record their responses. Some children will be able to write on their own, spelling as best they can with invented spelling. Others will rely on a grown-up to serve as their scribe, recording their ideas. These challenges will build concepts and vocabulary and provide opportunities for children to see themselves as writers. The oral version of this activity is appropriate for children aged 2½ and up, the written form for children 4 and over.

### MATERIALS TO GATHER

The easiest way to prepare for this activity is to create a form and duplicate as many copies as needed. (See example at right.) The simple form contains a rectangular box at the top in which the grown-up writes the category. Underneath appears a list of blank spaces, numbered 1 to 10. Depending on the age and interest of the children, any or all of the following categories might be appropriate: fairy tales, colors, ice-cream flavors, vehicles, desserts, toys, things to draw with, songs you know, things in the sky, things in the ocean, insects, fruit, girls' names, boys' names, healthy snacks, cereals, beverages, ways to move your body, ways to travel, vegetables, jungle animals, flowers, farm animals, kinds of jobs, and articles of clothing.

### INVITATIONS TO PLAY

◆ This activity can be introduced orally, with no pencil and paper needed. Move on to written form if children keep repeating the same words.

I have an idea for a simple game. Can you name ten colors? I will count with my fingers, raising one each time you think of another color.

◆ If children keep repeating the same colors, suggest the value of writing the words down.

> It's hard to remember if you said that color already—I'd better write the names of the colors down so we will know which ones you have already said. This is a special form I prepared to write down what you say.

◆ Always write so that the children can see the words as you write them, with the letters facing right-side up as the children look at them. Sound each word out slowly, inviting children to call out any letters they think are needed to spell the words.

> The first color you named is red, so I am going to write it right here next to number 1. Do you know what letter I should write down first?
>
> Yes, we use an *r* to make the sound at the beginning of *red*.
>
> Then we use an *e*. What do you hear at the end?
>
> Yes, we use the letter *d* for the final sound in *red*.

◆ Initial consonant sounds and final consonant sounds are easier for young children to hear than medial (middle) vowel sounds, such as the *a* in *cat*.

◆ If children are not yet ready to connect letters to sounds, spell the word on your own as you say it slowly, making sure to say the sounds at the same time you write the corresponding letter.

◆ If children are comfortable writing on their own, explain the form to them and provide pencils or markers. Celebrate all efforts to generate responses and to spell them.

◆ If children cannot think of ten responses for any category, be ready to provide additional ones.

◆ Read the list aloud upon completion. Celebrate the children's hard work.

◆ If children are interested, suggest another category and ask them to "name ten."

## TIPS TO CONSIDER

◆ This activity can be carried out without prepared forms; simply place the category at the top of a blank sheet of paper, and write the numbers 1 through 10 down the left side of the page. Children do, however, seem to delight in the "grown-up" use of forms, particularly if the paper is a surprising color. Special paper seems to elevate the status of the work.

◆ Include as many categories as you can think of. Be sure they are of interest to the children.

◆ Think of invented spelling as the way folks minimize the number of letters in telegrams to save money. Children usually begin with initial consonant sounds, then add final ones. Vowels follow, with long vowels appearing before short ones.

◆ Young children often mistakenly, yet cleverly, rely on the names of letters to help them guess beginning sounds. For example, don't be surprised if youngsters guess that the word *children* begins with the letter *h*. Children often choose the letter whose name /ait<u>ch</u>/ seems closest to the sound they are seeking. Similarly, they might guess that the word *elephant* begins with an *l* or the word *watermelon* begins with a *y*.

◆ Always encourage beginning writers to stretch words out slowly so that they hear more sounds.

◆ The category makes it easier for grown-ups to successfully read children's invented spellings. For example, if the category is ice cream flavors and children write "VNLA," "STRBRE," and "HKLT," you will be able to guess that the children are attempting to write "vanilla," "strawberry," and "chocolate."

## POSSIBILITIES TO EXTEND THE LEARNING

• Invite children to challenge family members with Name Ten sheets, and encourage them to generate additional categories.

• Name Ten is a game that results in lists of words. Children can also be invited to write lists for lots of real-world reasons, including shopping, party guests, and holiday gift requests. Demonstrate how writing lists also helps people remember important things. For example, work with children to create a list as they pack for a sleepover at Grandma's or prepare for a birthday party. The example at right shows a list of house rules for a new babysitter begun by a parent and completed by a child. The child's invented spelling reads, "Have treats after meals have been eaten" and "Children may not be alone in the bath."

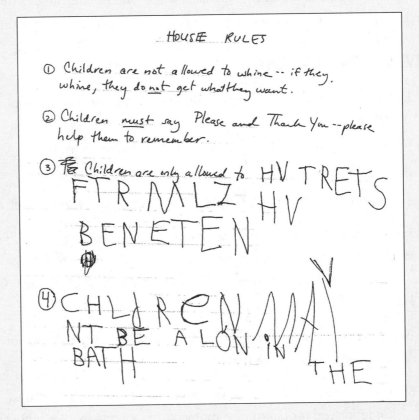

• In addition to lists, children can be encouraged to write labels, letters, signs, surveys, maps, reminders, invitations, thank-you notes, and stories. (See Family Survey, page 132. See also Mini-Museum on page 137 for more information on beginning writing attempts.)

# 45. Doctor Play

*ACCOMPLISHMENTS: engaging in dramatic play, appreciating the role writing plays in the real world, using invented spelling to support play*

As noted in the other dramatic play activities in this book (Clothing Store Shopkeeper, page 105, and Mini-Museum, page 137, children learn a number of social and communication skills when they engage in pretend situations. In addition, they increase their knowledge of vocabulary and concepts connected to the area of play. In playing doctor, children can be encouraged to write for all the reasons that doctors write. Here, they are asked to write prescriptions. This activity is appropriate for all children who engage in dramatic play and are interested in taking pen to paper. Some will pretend-write, while others will use invented spelling, moving on to standard spelling when they are ready.

## MATERIALS TO GATHER

A pad of paper and a marker for writing prescriptions are all that is needed for this dramatic play activity. Some children may choose to use other props, including an adult white shirt as a lab coat, a toy stethoscope, a spoon to check for bouncing knee reflexes, and other pretend medical supplies. Dolls may also support the dramatic play.

## INVITATIONS TO PLAY

◆ If children don't initiate playing doctor, you could make the suggestion.

   Oh, no! I think your doll has a cold just like the one you had last week. I'd better take her to the doctor. You can be the doctor, and I'll be the baby's mom. Okay?

◆ Once children have examined the doll, be sure to ask for a prescription.

   So, doctor, what do you suggest I do to help my baby feel better?

◆ Encourage the children to write down a prescription on their pads. Repeat the prescription slowly for the children so they can hear more sounds.

   So you think I should give her lots of juice and chicken soup. Could you write that down so I won't forget?

◆ Be accepting of children's invented spelling. Don't be surprised if children's attempts at writing "juice" and "chicken soup" read "JS" and "HKN SP."

◆ Show children that you can read the words, and celebrate their hard work.

   Good for you for hearing so many of the sounds in *juice* and *chicken soup*.
   Now you can say, "Next, please," and I will bring in the next patient.
   This time my baby has diaper rash. What should I do?

◆ Once again, after the "doctors" examine the pretend patients, encourage the children to write prescriptions.

   So you think I should use Vaseline and Desitin cream? Please give me a prescription.

◆ Once again, help children to hear more sounds by saying the words slowly and encouraging them to write down the letters needed.

◆ Be accepting of children's attempts, and show them that you can read their words.

Yes, those letters ("*VSLN*") tell me to use Vaseline and those letters ("*DSTN*") tell me to use Desitin.

◆ At some point, reverse roles, writing prescriptions by sounding words out slowly in front of the children.

◆ Continue playing doctor until children need a change in activity.

## TIPS TO CONSIDER

◆ Children may not be ready to use invented spelling. Be accepting of their pretend writing (up and down mountain peaks, long lines of loops) or even random letters with no connection to the sounds of the words being suggested.

◆ Understand why *chicken* might be spelled as "HKN." As mentioned in the Name Ten activity (page 127), beginning writers often record the sound of /ch/ with just an *h* because they associate that sound with the name of the letter—"aitch." Then, too, beginning writers often write words with beginning and final consonants alone, adding vowel sounds at a later stage.

◆ When you write in front of children, you need not write in invented spelling. You can use standard spelling, but still say the words slowly so that you are writing the letters as you are making the sounds. Children will learn a great deal from your demonstration.

## POSSIBILITIES TO EXTEND THE LEARNING

• Expand the number of literacy-related props when playing doctor, adding such things as eye charts, health records, appointment pads, and even reading material in the waiting room.

• Add literacy events to other kinds of dramatic play, including playing restaurant, veterinarian's office, supermarket, lemonade stand, toy store, and library.

• Whenever possible, use real-world objects to support children's play, including subscription order forms, outdated checkbooks, book orders, and telephone and address books.

• Read related picture books, including *Alexander's Pretending Day* by Bunny Crumpacker, *Next Please* by Ernst Jandl, and *Froggy Goes to the Doctor* by Jonathan London.

# 46. Family Survey

*ACCOMPLISHMENTS: learning sight words, using invented spelling, appreciating surveys*

Children love to feel as if they are doing grown-up work, especially if the results of their work make a difference in their lives. In this activity, children are asked to take family surveys, the results of which are actually put to good use. Children will come to understand the basics of surveys, receive practice in tallying results, and learn sight words along the way. This activity is appropriate for children aged 4 and up.

## MATERIALS TO GATHER

Paper and pencil are all that is needed for this activity. The survey can be created in front of the children to demonstrate its use. In this case, names of people are written at the top of columns and choices are listed down the left-hand side of the lined paper. (See example at right.)

| PASTA | Mom | Dad | Andie | Will | Maria | Grandpa | Grandma |
|---|---|---|---|---|---|---|---|
| Ravioli | | | ✓ | | | | |
| Tortellini | | | | ✓ | | | |
| Spaghetti | ✓ | | | | | | |
| Macaroni | | | | | | | |
| Angel Hair | | ✓ | | | ✓ | ✓ | |
| Linguini | | | | | | | |
| Penne | | | | | | | ✓ |

## INVITATIONS TO PLAY

◆ Introduce the idea of surveys to children, suggesting why a survey might be helpful.

We're going to have pasta for dinner tomorrow night, but I can't decide which kind to make. Maybe we should survey all the people in the family, asking each of them about their favorite pasta, and that will help us decide which one to prepare.

◆ Demonstrate how to prepare a survey form.

I'm going to draw five columns, and at the top of each one, I am going to write the name of one person in the family. Then along the left side of the page, I am going to list all the different pasta dishes we love to prepare, one on each line.

◆ Encourage children to suggest pasta dishes. Write the names of the dishes, spelling them out slowly.

So far we have: spaghetti and meatballs, macaroni and cheese, spinach tortellini, cheese ravioli, meat lasagna. We'll just write the names of the noodles to save space.

◆ Consider adding simple illustrations to help children read the names of the pasta dishes and the names of family members.

◆ Describe how to take a survey.

Now your job will be to take the survey. That means you have to ask every member of the family which of these pasta dishes is their favorite. You will have to read the list aloud to them and then check off the one they choose.

I added my name to the survey, so why don't you begin with me?

Read the list to me and I will tell you which my favorite is. Then I will show you how to put a check next to that dish in the column that has my name.

◆ Describe how to tally the survey results.

When we have asked everyone and you have added your vote, we will count the votes and the dish that has the most votes will be the one I cook for dinner tomorrow night.

## TIPS TO CONSIDER

◆ If this activity is being conducted at school, consider survey topics such as authors to study, field trips to take, snacks to share, or songs to learn.

◆ Be sure to make the survey count. In other words, explain the reason for conducting the survey and then put the results to real use.

◆ If children have begun to spell on their own, invite them to write the names and items as best they can on survey forms.

◆ Keep family surveys in a safe place. They will bring back precious memories to all members of the family.

## POSSIBILITIES TO EXTEND THE LEARNING

• Other possibilities for surveys done at home include choosing which soup to prepare, restaurant to eat in, playground to visit, cookie to bake, color to paint living room walls, and movie to watch.

• Whenever real-world surveys arrive in the mail, be sure to share them with children.

• In addition to surveys, create important check-off lists as a means of helping children to become organized and prepared. For example, you can create a weekly check-off with the days of the week across the top and a list of things to do to get ready in the morning appearing in a column down the left side of the page. Separate items with straight lines, creating a grid. After completing each chore, children should be encouraged to check off such items as "brush teeth," "eat breakfast," "wash hands and face," and "get dressed." A similar check-off can be created to help with bedtime.

# 47. Homemade Books

*ACCOMPLISHMENTS: using invented spelling, labeling pictures, writing captions, learning sight words*

Homemade books created for and/or by children become precious family heirlooms. In this activity, adults help children label family photographs and create their own book of favorite things. Children begin by memorizing the labeled pictures, learning words on sight as they reread the books. Other suggestions for homemade books are offered in Possibilities to Extend the Learning. This activity is appropriate for all children, with adults doing more of the cutting, drawing, and writing for the youngest children.

## MATERIALS TO GATHER

This activity requires a collection of family snapshots. Schoolchildren can be asked to bring in photographs from home. In addition, small self-sticking labels, a pen or marker, some crayons for decorating the title page, and a blank 4-by 6-inch photo album are needed.

## INVITATIONS TO PLAY

◆ Invite children to browse collections of family photos. (If photos are already in albums, some will need to be removed to create these special books for the children.)

Let's take some time today to look at old photos. Can you make a stack of photos that show the people or places or things that you especially love?

◆ Encourage children to choose items that can be easily named.

You chose such perfect photographs because you do love your mom, your dad, your brother, Will, your sister, Sasha, and your cousins Ben and Zach.

And of course, you love your friends Hannah, Jordyn, and Alexandra.

And these are great choices because you do love pizza, Play-Doh, your sippy cup, and monkey bread.

And I know how much you love to bake cookies, go to the playground, and draw.

◆ Suggest putting selected photos in a special album.

I think you are old enough to have your very own photo album, one that shows all the things that you love.

◆ Help children slip photos into the sleeves of their albums. Leave the first sleeve blank to create a title page.

Let's think of a good title for this book that is filled with all the things you love.

◆ Be accepting of children's title suggestions.

Yes, we can call it "Andie's I Love Book," and you can decorate this page any way you'd like.

◆ Using small self-sticking labels, create the title page and captions for each photograph.

Let's pretend you are talking in this book. What would you say about this first photograph?

- Record children's ideas, but be sure to use simple repetitive phrases. This will facilitate children's recall and "reading" of the words.

> Yes, it makes sense to write, "I love my mommy."
>
> And what should I write on this page?

- Continue labeling each page.

> "I love my Daddy."
>
> "I love my brother, Will."
>
> "I love my sister, Sasha."
>
> "I love my cousin Ben."
>
> "I love my cousin Zach."
>
> "I love my friend Hannah."
>
> "I love my friend Jordyn."
>
> "I love my friend Alexandra."

- When all photos are labeled, read the book aloud to the children.

- Encourage children to then read aloud to you, reminding them that the pictures will help them remember what the words say.

- Suggest the importance of taking care of the book and rereading it often.

> Let's be sure to keep this book in a very special place so that the photos and the words will be safe and you can read the book to yourself whenever you choose.

## TIPS TO CONSIDER

- Write slowly in front of children so that they can hear you say the sounds of the words as you are writing the letters.

- If children do not have sufficient photos, invite them to draw the things they love.

- When children are ready to use invented spelling, invite them to do the writing as best they can. Most young children need bigger spaces for writing, so larger albums with room for larger labels will be necessary.

### POSSIBILITIES TO EXTEND THE LEARNING

Fill a bookshelf with homemade books. A few ideas follow.

- Create a special-event photo book. For example, you might label scenes from family weddings or holiday parties, asking the children to narrate the events.

- Create original toy books, by clipping photographs from toy catalogs. Glue a picture of one toy to every page, printing the name of the toy and any comments made by the children.

- Create original counting books, writing the numbers 1 to 20 in a blank book, one number per page. Invite the children to draw items and/or clip magazine photos to correspond with each number. Label the items.

- As suggested on page 77, help children turn well-known songs into picture books.

- As suggested on page 91, help children create original neighborhood guidebooks.

- As suggested on page 110, help children create original picture books of neighborhood street signs.

- As suggested on page 74, help children create original alphabet books by taking photographs of their favorite things or inviting them to prepare illustrations for each letter of the alphabet.

- As suggested on page 18, help children create original "teaching" books about their main areas of interest.

# 48. Mini-Museum

*ACCOMPLISHMENTS: learning new vocabulary, engaging in dramatic play,*
*appreciating labels, signs, ads, maps, etc.*

Children are born collectors. In this activity, they are challenged to bring order to their collections while they learn new vocabulary, appreciate the work that takes place in a museum, and value the role reading and writing play in museum exhibits. Then, too, children have ample opportunity to engage in dramatic play, fostering their social and communication skills. This activity is appropriate for children aged 3½ and up.

## MATERIALS TO GATHER

This activity depends on children's collections, the kinds of things they stash in shoeboxes under their beds or in a special corner of a toy chest or dresser drawer. Depending on the contents of the collection (rocks, shells, leaves, etc.), an informational book that identifies the items could be helpful, but it is not essential. Some children collect things that do not have specific names attached to them, such as erasers, buttons, or stickers. These items would be just as appropriate for a Mini-Museum exhibit and could be sorted by size, color, or texture. You'll need writing and drawing materials for various signs, advertisements, brochures, maps, tickets, and labels. You'll also need shoebox covers or serving trays to display items.

## INVITATIONS TO PLAY

◆ Introduce the activity.

Do you remember when we visited the American Museum of Natural History and we saw all those dinosaur bones and all those totem poles and all those beautiful masks? Well, I think we can create our own little museum with all your favorite collections. What do you think we could display?

◆ If children have no ideas, remind them of their collections.

Well, I think you have enough rocks, shells, and leaves to set up a small museum.

◆ Ask children to gather all their artifacts.

Can you put all your shells, rocks, and leaves in one place?

◆ Help children decide how they will organize them.

You have to be the museum curator now. That means you are the person who plans the exhibits.

You can use these trays to display your rocks. How do you want to organize them? Do you want to sort them by color, by size, by how they feel? What other way might they be placed on the tray so that the people who visit your museum will appreciate them?

◆ Help children place rocks in the tray according to the sorting system they have chosen.

Now we should label them so people know what they are looking at. We could write "big rocks," "medium rocks," and "small rocks."

- If you have a guidebook and enough variety among the rocks you could attempt to identify them.

  Let's try to find them in this guidebook so we can write the name next to each rock.

- Write labels and names for children if they are not ready to do so.

- Help children present other collections in a similar way, identifying them if possible.

  Now let's organize your shells, and then we will do your leaves.

- When all collections are arranged, invite children to prepare the museum for visitors.

  What can we do to make this seem more like a real museum?

- If children have no ideas, you might make some suggestions. Many suggestions will lead to writing and/or drawing tasks. Young children will need help completing these. Consider the written work as teamwork, inviting children to do as much as they can.

  Do you think we need a name for our museum? If you choose one, we can make and hang a sign.

  Do you think the neighbors know about your museum? Perhaps we should make an advertisement and hang it on our front door.

  Will you be selling tickets? We'd better design those.

  Do you think people will need a map so they know where to find the exhibits? How can we draw a map?

  How about some information about each exhibit? People might want to know where you got all these things. We can hang a little label next to each exhibit with that kind of information.

- When written work is complete, invite children to use the museum for their dramatic play.

  What job do you want in the museum?

- If children have no responses, offer them possibilities.

  You've been the curator, but now you can be the guide who shows visitors around or the museum visitor who wants to learn about your collections or the security guard who keeps the collections safe, or the cashier who sells the tickets.

- Take turns playing different roles, then invite family members to visit the museum and join in the dramatic play.

## TIPS TO CONSIDER

- Whenever visiting museums, take home handouts to use as models.

- Allow children to create the kind of museum that matches their main areas of interest, including such topics as fire vehicles, dolls, or toy dinosaurs.

- If children are interested and ready, allow them to make museum signs, labels, tickets, and other written material using invented spelling or even pretend writing. (See page 127 for more information on beginning writing.)

## POSSIBILITIES TO EXTEND THE LEARNING

- Share nonfiction books on children's favorite collections.

- Create art museums using children's original works of art. Ask children to create galleries of their work, adding titles and signatures to each piece. Help children to mount cards alongside each piece, listing the medium used, the date completed, and the location in which the work was done, much as you would see in an art museum. Create museum artifacts (tickets, brochures, signs, and so on) to encourage dramatic play.

- Demonstrate the labels you write for real-world reasons, including those on buckets of toys and art supplies, photo albums and frozen-food containers. Invite children to help write the words if they are ready.

- Read *Hannah's Collections* by Marthe Jocelyn.

- Sing "Collecting Bottle Caps" and "The Toy Museum" from Laurie Berkner's CD, *Victor Vito* (Two Tomatoes Records).

- Read picture books about museums, including *How to Take Your Grandmother to the Museum* by Lois Wyse and Molly Rose Goldman and *Matthew's Dream* by Leo Lionni, as well as the poetry collection *Behind the Museum Door: Poems to Celebrate the Wonder of Museums*, edited by Lee Bennett Hopkins.

# 49. Spelling Fun

*ACCOMPLISHMENTS: using known words to spell new words*

The first word children usually learn to spell is their name. They can often recite the letters in proper sequence before they can print them on their own. In the activities described below, the spelling of words is woven joyfully into everyday interactions, songs, playtimes, and conversations. This activity is appropriate for children aged 3 and up.

## MATERIALS TO GATHER

This beginning spelling activity centers on singing song lyrics that spell out words. These include the traditional song "Bingo," the theme song of the television program *Mickey Mouse Clubhouse*, and an original song called "Boots" on Laurie Berkner's CD *Victor Vito*. In addition, a wipe-off board, dry-erase marker, and eraser—or paper and pencil or marker—will come in handy.

## INVITATIONS TO PLAY

◆ Begin by singing the popular children's song "Bingo."

> Let's sing that song about the farmer who had a dog named Bingo.
>
> There was a farmer had a dog,
> And Bingo was his name, oh!
> B-I-N-G-O.
> B-I-N-G-O.
> B-I-N-G-O.
> And Bingo was his name, oh!

◆ Suggest recording the spelling of the dog's name on the dry-erase board or on a slip of paper.

> This time when we sing it, I'll write the letters down so that we can see what the word *Bingo* looks like.

◆ Suggest that the word *Bingo* can help us spell and read other words.

> This word is *Bingo*. What happens if I change the *B* to an *R*?
> Yes, it spells *Ringo*.
> What if I change the first letter to a *D* or a *Z* or a *W*?

◆ Sing the song again, this time having fun substituting the new words.

> There was a farmer had a dog,
> And Ringo was his name, oh!
> R-I-N-G-O . . .

◆ Continue singing the song by substituting other rhyming names.

◆ Show children that the *i-n-g* in *Bingo* is a very useful group of letters to know.

> If we take off the letter *o* from the end of *Bingo*, the word is *Bing*.
>
> If we take off the *B* at the beginning of the word the letters make the sound /ing/.
>
> And *i-n-g* is a very useful group of letters to know.

◆ Show children how the rime *-ing* can help form many new words.

> Let's put different letters in front of *-ing* and see what words we make.

◆ Write such rhyming words as *sing, king, ring*.

◆ If children are still interested in looking at words, you can add that *-ing* also comes at the end of many words.

> Sometimes when you are looking at books you will see the letters *i-n-g* at the end of words, like in *walking, eating*, and *playing*.

◆ On another occasion, if the songs are familiar to children, you can play in a similar way with the television anthem "Mickey Mouse" ("M-I-C-K-E-Y. . . M-O-U-S-E"), and Laurie Berkner's song "Boots" ("B-O-O-T-S").

## TIPS TO CONSIDER

◆ If children are not ready to recall the spelling of words, postpone this activity until a later time.

◆ If you're using "Mickey Mouse," you can rhyme words with *Mick* as well as *Mickey*, as *-ick* is a very helpful rime to know. Don't worry if some of the substitutions of initial letters form nonsense words. Children will enjoy playing with the sounds.

> *Mick, sick, lick, nick, trick, slick, stick*
> *mouse, house, louse, blouse*

(Some of the beginning sounds of the rhyming words require two letters, blending two sounds together. These words will be harder for many children to spell.)

### POSSIBILITIES TO EXTEND THE LEARNING

• List all the words children recognize on sight and demonstrate to children how knowing these can help them read and write others. For example, if children know that *S-T-O-P* spells the word *stop*, ask them how they might spell the words *hop, pop*, and *top*.

• Look around the house or classroom for words that the children see frequently. Increase children's visual memory and spelling ability by asking them to look, for example, at the word *milk* on their milk containers.

Can you look carefully at the word *milk* and try to remember how to spell the word? Now cover your eyes and tell me what letters spell *milk*. Open your eyes and see if you were right.

If children can't recall the letters, ask them to study the word again and try to spell it without looking at the container. Be sure the letters are offered in the correct order. Repeat with other words in the environment. Ask children to write the letters down if they are able.

- Try spelling out secret messages. Whenever appropriate or helpful, try spelling messages to older children so that the youngest ones won't know what you are saying. For example, when a cranky baby wakes up, you might say to older children:

  I think the baby looks *S-A-D*.
  I think he needs an *H-U-G*.

  Other home situations might demand that you ask the following:
  Is it time for the baby's *B-A-T-H*?
  Maybe I should give him a *B-O-T-T-L-E*.
  Do you want *P-I-Z-Z-A* for dinner?

  At school you might offer the following spellings out loud.
  Do you think that it is time for our *S-N-A-C-K*?
  Let's pick a good *B-O-O-K*.
  Tomorrow is a very special *D-A-Y*.

  Tell children the words you are spelling out loud and they will begin to remember them.

- Once children can spell a few words, teach them to play a variation on the traditional Hangman game called Beat the Clock. When children guess the wrong letters, fill in the numbers on a clock face instead of completing the drawing of a man being hanged. In addition to being nonviolent, the game teaches children the position of numbers on the clock. The game is over once all the numbers are filled in or the word is spelled.

- Invite children to freely explore with sets of Scrabble tiles and/or magnetic letters. Celebrate when they attempt to read their creations.

- Use familiar book titles to help children determine the spelling of additional words. For example, if they can read *Hop on Pop*, ask them to spell such words as *top*, *mop*, *crop*, and *stop*.

Look Who's Learning to Read

# 50. "Naughty" Notes

*ACCOMPLISHMENTS: reading environmental print, appreciating how additions and deletions of letters can change the meaning of words*

It's not just at Halloween that children delight in tricks and treats. In this reading and writing activity, children take pleasure in "tricking" grown-ups by changing the print in lists, letters, and reminders found around the house or classroom. They learn how adding letters to the beginning or end of words creates new words and how adding or deleting words can change the meaning of messages, often with humorous results. This activity is appropriate for children who are beginning to recognize words on sight and understand how to form new words from known ones. Adults can do the writing for children who are not yet ready to do so.

## MATERIALS TO GATHER

This activity requires gathering short notes, lists, reminders, or other printed material found around the home or in the classroom.

## INVITATIONS TO PLAY

◆ Read aloud a text of interest to the children. It might be a shopping list, a recipe, a reminder, a request, or an announcement. Select one that lends itself to a bit of "tampering."

This is the recipe for baking sugar cookies that we used last week.

Let's look at the list of ingredients. Do you recognize any of them?

◆ Introduce the activity.

Would you like to do some funny writing? We could change some of the words around to create a silly recipe.

◆ Demonstrate how adding letters or words changes meaning.

Watch what happens when I add some letters or words.

Like here, where it says "one egg," let's add the words "salad sandwich."

Now the cookie recipe calls for one egg salad sandwich. Isn't that silly?

◆ Invite children's participation.

And here it reads, "one teaspoon of vanilla." What could we change that to?

Yes, we could write the words "ice cream" after the word "vanilla." That would surely change this recipe. What else might we do? What could we add after "one cup butter"? How about changing it to "one cup buttered popcorn"? That would really make a ridiculous recipe.

◆ Continue altering the baking directions.

Now let's look at the directions.

Here it says, "Sift together flour, baking soda and baking powder." What happens if I slip an "s" in front of "and"? Yes, it now reads "Sift together flour, baking soda, sand baking powder."

Oh, that sounds awful! We would never put sand in our cookies.

Here it says, "Cool on wire racks." What if we slipped a "t" in front of "racks"? Yes, it now reads, "tracks." Should we cool our cookies on train tracks or moose tracks?

Here it says, "Roll dough into balls." What word could we put before "balls" to make this recipe really sound silly? Yes, we could write "meatballs," "snowballs," or even "baseballs."

◆ Make sure to inform children that you are not really trying to be mischievous.

Do you think anyone would fall for our silly recipe? Do you think anyone would think that this is a real recipe? No, I think people would just laugh.

I think they would know we were just playing with words and letters.

## TIPS TO CONSIDER

◆ Make sure that children know that this activity is just for fun, and that altering important messages on their own, without permission, could cause problems.

◆ Some children may want to slip in letters all over the page you share, creating many nonsense words. Be accepting of children's interest, but do explain that adding letters to the page doesn't necessarily create real words. Read back the nonsense words the children create. For some children, this may be funny enough.

## POSSIBILITIES TO EXTEND THE LEARNING

- Have fun altering shopping lists. Show children how an original list can become a totally different one with the addition of just a few letters and words.

    **Milk** ➜ **Milk**y Way candy bars

    **salt** ➜ **salt**y pretzels

    **sugar** ➜ **sugar** cones

    **cheese** ➜ **cheese**burgers

- Have fun altering reminders, sharing with children how different and often silly the message can become with just a few changes in letters and words.

    **Clean car** ➜ **Clean** scar

    **Buy ink** ➜ **Buy** sinks

    **Change oil in car** ➜ **Change** soil in car

    **Defrost fish** ➜ **Defrost fish**ing rods

    **Return library books on Tuesday** ➜ **Return library book**shelf **on Tuesday**

    **Make appointment with doctor** ➜ **Make appointment with**out **doctor**

- Whenever leaving messages around the home or classroom, be sure to write them using legible print so that children will attempt to read them.

# Favorite Read-Alouds

The titles that follow are some of our favorite read-alouds. Ask your librarian or bookseller for other books by these authors, as space constraints make it impossible to list every worthwhile title. Then too, folk and fairy tales have been omitted from these lists as so many wonderful versions are available. A list of classic stories appears on page 157 of this Appendix. Although the books listed below are primarily works of fiction, with an occasional poetry or nonfiction title slipped in, poems and informational texts should form an integral part of any read-aloud repertoire. A list of poets and nonfiction writers for very young children appears on page 156.

In addition, do not feel limited by the suggested age spans attached to each list. Children can enjoy books listed for younger or older listeners, especially if they appeal to their tastes or interests. As children get older and their attention spans increase, add chapter books to your read-alouds and aim to get children hooked on favorite series.

Note as well that the titles recommended within each activity are *not* included here, but are included in the Works Cited list beginning on page 158.

## 2- to 3-Year-Olds

Alborough, Jez. *Duck in the Truck*. New York: HarperCollins, 2000.

Arnosky, Jim. *Crinkleroot's Mammals Every Child Should Know*. Tarrytown, NY: Bradbury Press, 1994.

Asch, Frank. *Barnyard Animals*. New York: Aladdin, 1998.

Bang, Molly. *Ten, Nine, Eight*. New York: Greenwillow, 1983.

Bang, Molly. *Yellow Ball*. New York: Morrow Junior, 1991.

Barchas, Sarah E. *I Was Walking Down the Road*. Illustrated by Jack Kent. New York: Scholastic, 1975.

Beaumont, Karen. *Duck, Duck, Goose! (A Coyote's on the Loose!)*. Illustrated by Jose Aruego and Ariane Dewey. New York: HarperCollins, 2004.

Bergman, Mara. *Snip Snap! What's That?* Illustrated by Nick Maland. New York: Greenwillow, 2005.

Borden, Louise. *Caps, Hats, Socks and Mittens: A Book About the Four Seasons*. Illustrated by Lillian Hoban. New York: Scholastic, 1989.

Boynton, Sandra. *The Going to Bed Book*. New York: Little Simon, 1982.

Brown, Margaret Wise. *Big Red Barn*. Illustrated by Felicia Bond. New York: HarperCollins, 1989.

Browne, Anthony. *My Mom*. New York: Farrar, Straus and Giroux, 2005.

Bunting, Eve. *Little Bear's Little Boat*. Illustrated by Nancy Carpenter, New York: Clarion, 2007.

Butler, John. *Can You Growl Like a Bear?* Atlanta, GA: Peachtree Publishers, 2007.

Campbell, Rod. *Dear Zoo*. New York: Little Simon, 2005.

Carle, Eric. *From Head to Toe*. New York: HarperCollins, 1997.

Carle, Eric. *Have You Seen My Cat?* New York: Simon & Schuster, 1997.

Carr, Jan. *Dappled Apples*. Illustrated by Dorothy Donahue. New York: Holiday House, 2001.

Carr, Jan. *Frozen Noses*. Illustrated by Dorothy Donahue. New York: Holiday House, 1999.

Carr, Jan. *Splish, Splash, Spring*. Illustrated by Dorothy Donahue. New York: Holiday House, 2001.

Christelow, Eileen. *Five Little Monkeys Jumping on the Bed*. New York: Scholastic, 1989.

Crews, Donald. *Freight Train*. New York: Greenwillow, 1978.

Crews, Donald. *Ten Black Dots*. New York: Greenwillow, 1986.

de Regniers, Beatrice Schenk. *What Can You Do with a Shoe?* Illustrated by Maurice Sendak. New York: Harper & Row, 1955.

de Regniers, Beatrice Schenk. *What Did You Put in Your Pocket?* Illustrated by Michael Grejniec. New York: HarperCollins, 2003.

Donaldson, Julia. *The Gruffalo*. Illustrated by Alex Scheffler. New York: Macmillan, 1999.

Downing, Julie. *Where Is My Mommy?* New York: HarperCollins, 2003.

Dr. Seuss. *ABC: An Amazing Alphabet Book!* New York: Random House, 1996.

Dr. Seuss. *The Cat in the Hat*. New York: Random House, 1957.

Dr. Seuss. *Green Eggs and Ham*. New York: Random House, 1960.

Dr. Seuss. *Hop on Pop*. New York: Random House, 1963.

Dr. Seuss. *One Fish, Two Fish, Red Fish, Blue Fish*. New York: Random House, 1960.

Duncan, Pamela. *Wake Up Kisses*. Illustrated by Henry Cole. New York: HarperCollins, 2001.

Eastman, P. D. *Big Dog…Little Dog: A Bedtime Story*. New York: Random House, 1973.

Ericsson, Jennifer A. *No Milk!* Illustrated by Ora Eitan. New York: Tambourine Books, 1993.

Fleming, Denise. *In the Small, Small Pond*. New York: Henry Holt, 1993.

Florian, Douglas. *A Pig Is Big*. New York: Greenwillow, 2000.

Foley, Greg. *Thank You Bear*. New York: Viking, 2007.

Fox, Mem. *Boo to a Goose*. Illustrated by David Miller. New York: Puffin, 1996.

Fox, Mem. *Hattie and the Fox*. Illustrated by Patricia Mullins. New York: Ashton Scholastic, 1986.

Fox, Mem. *Time for Bed*. Illustrated by Jane Dyer. New York: Scholastic, 1993.

Fox, Mem. *Where Is the Green Sheep?* Illustrated by Judy Horacek. New York: Harcourt, 2004.

Fox, Mem. *Zoo-Looking*. Illustrated by Rodney McRae. New York: Scholastic, 1986.

Guarino, Deborah. *Is Your Mama a Llama?* Illustrated by Steven Kellogg, New York: Scholastic, 1989.

Hachler, Bruno. *What Does My Teddy Bear Do All Day?* Illustrated by Birte Muller. Translated by Charise Myngheer. New York: Penguin, 2004.

Hayes, Sarah. *This Is the Bear*. Illustrated by Helen Craig. Cambridge. MA: Candlewick Press, 1986.

Henkes, Kevin. *A Good Day*. New York: HarperCollins, 2007.

Hoberman, Mary Ann. *One of Each*. Illustrated by Marjorie Priceman, New York: Little, Brown, 1997.

Hutchins, Pat. *Barn Dance*. New York: Greenwillow, 2007.

Isadora, Rachel. *Bring on That Beat*. New York: G. P. Putnam's Sons, 2004.

Johnson, Crockett. *Harold and the Purple Crayon*. New York: HarperCollins, 1955.

Johnson, Stephen. *Alphabet City*. New York: Viking, 1995.

Karas, G. Brian, illus. *Skidamarink—A Silly Love Song to Sing Together*. New York: HarperCollins, 2002.

Kirk, David. *Miss Spider's Tea Party*. New York: Scholastic, 1994.

Kuskin, Karla. *Green as a Bean*. Illustrated by Melissa Iwai. New York: HarperCollins, 2007.

Lillegard, Dee. *Balloons, Balloons, Balloons*. Illustrated by Bernadette Pons. New York: Dutton, 2007.

Lionni, Leo. *Little Blue and Little Yellow*. New York: HarperCollins, 1959.

Lobel, Anita. *One Lighthouse, One Moon*. New York: Greenwillow, 2000.

London, Jonathan. *Crunch, Munch*. Illustrated by Michael Rex. New York: Harcourt, 2001.

Mahy, Margaret. *A Lion in the Meadow*. New York: Puffin, 1989.

Martin Jr., Bill. *Brown Bear, Brown Bear, What Do You See?* Illustrated by Eric Carle. New York: Holt, Rinehart and Winston, 1967.

Marzollo, Jean. *Pretend You're a Cat*. Illustrated by Jerry Pinkney. New York: Dial Books for Young Readers, 1990.

Miranda, Anne. *To Market, to Market*. Illustrated by Janet Stevens. New York: Harcourt, 2007.

Pumphrey, Jerome, and Jarrett Pumphrey. *Creepy Things Are Scaring Me*. Illustrated by Rosanne Litzinger. New York: HarperCollins, 2005.

Purmell, Ann. *Where Wild Babies Sleep*. Illustrated by Lorianne Siomades. Honesdale, PA: Boyds Mills Press, 2003.

Raffi. *Down by the Bay*. Illustrated by Nadine Bernard Westcott. New York: Random House, 1987.

Rex, Michael. *Dunk Skunk*. New York: G. P. Putnam's Sons, 2005.

Rex, Michael. *Truck Duck*. New York: G. P. Putnam's Sons, 2004.

Riley, Linnea. *Mouse Mess*. New York: Blue Sky Press, 1997.

Robert, Bethany. *A Mouse Told His Mother*. Illustrated by Maryjane Begin. New York: Little, Brown, 1997.

Rockwell, Anne, and Harlow Rockwell. *The Toolbox*. New York: Macmillan, 1971.

Rosen, Michael. *We're Going on a Bear Hunt*. Illustrated by Helen Oxenbury. New York: Aladdin, 2003.

Rothstein, Gloria. *Sheep Asleep*. Illustrated by Lizzy Rockwell. New York: HarperCollins, 2003.

Ryder, Joanna. *Won't You Be My Kissaroo?* Illustrated by Melissa Sweet. New York: Harcourt, 2004.

Seeger, Laura Vaccaro. *First the Egg*. New Milford, CT: Roaring Brook Press, 2007.

Spinelli, Eileen. *When Mama Comes Home Tonight*. Illustrated by Jane Dyer. New York: Simon & Schuster, 1998.

Stadler, John. *One Seal*. New York: Orchard Books, 1999.

Steig, William. *Which Would You Rather Be?* Illustrated by Harry Bliss. New York: HarperCollins, 2002.

Sturges, Philomen. *How Do You Make a Baby Smile?* Illustrated by Bridget Strevens-Marzo. New York: HarperCollins, 2007.

Tafuri, Nancy. *The Busy Little Squirrel*. New York: Simon & Schuster, 2007.

Timmers, Leo. *Who Is Driving?* Translated by Clavis Uitgeverij. New York: Bloomsbury, 2007.

Van Laan, Nancy. *Teeny Tiny Tingly Tales*. Illustrated by Victoria Chess. New York: Atheneum, 2001.

Walton, Rick. *The Bear Came Over to My House*. Illustrated by James Warhola. New York: G. P. Putnam's Sons, 2001.

Walton, Sherry. *Books Are for Eating*. Illustrated by Nadine Bernard Westcott. New York: Dutton Juvenile, 1990.

Webb, Steve. *Tanka Tanka Skunk!* New York: Orchard Books, 2003.

Weeks, Sarah. *Mrs. McNosh Hangs Up Her Wash*. Illustrated by Nadine Bernard Westcott. New York: HarperCollins, 1998.

Wilson, Karma. *Moose Tracks*. Illustrated by Jack E. Davis. New York: Margaret K. McElderry Books, 2006.

Wood, Audrey. *The Napping House*. New York: Harcourt, 1984.

Wood, Audrey. *Piggies*. Illustrated by Don Wood. Orlando, FL: Voyager Books, 1997.

Wood, Audrey. *Silly Sally*. New York: Harcourt, 1992.

Yang, James. *Joey and Jet*. New York: Atheneum, 2004.

Yolen, Jane, and Heidi E. Y. Stemple. *Sleep, Black Bear, Sleep*. Illustrated by Brooke Dyer. New York: HarperCollins, 2007.

Ziefert, Harriet. *Amanda Zade's New Year's Parade*. Illustrated by S. D. Schindler. New York: Puffin, 1999.

Ziefert, Harriet. *Toes Have Wiggles, Kids Have Giggles*. New York: G. P. Putnam's Sons, 2002.

# 3- to 4-Year-Olds

Bauer, Marion Dane. *If You Were Born a Kitten*. Illustrated by JoEllen McAllister Stammen. New York: Simon & Schuster, 1997.

Bogart, Jo Ellen. *Gifts*. Illustrated by Barbara Reid. New York: Scholastic, 1994.

Bond, Rebecca. *The Great Doughnut Parade*. New York: Houghton Mifflin, 2007.

Browne, Anthony. *Silly Billy*. Cambridge, MA: Candlewick Press, 2006.

Bruel, Nick. *Bad Kitty*. New Milford, CT: Roaring Brook Press, 2005.

Bruel, Nick. *Poor Puppy*. New Milford, CT: Roaring Brook Press, 2007.

Bruss, Deborah. *Book! Book! Book!* Illustrated by Tiphanie Beeke. New York: Scholastic, 2001.

Cameron, Polly. *"I Can't," Said the Ant.* New York: Scholastic, 1961.

Carle, Eric. *Papa, Please Get the Moon for Me.* New York: Simon & Schuster, 1986.

Carle, Eric, illus. *Today Is Monday.* New York: Philomel, 1993.

Carlstrom, Nancy White. *Guess Who's Coming, Jesse Bear.* Illustrated by Bruce Degen. New York: Simon & Schuster, 1998.

Catalanotto, Peter. *Matthew A.B.C.* New York: Atheneum, 2002.

Crews, Nina. *The Neighborhood Mother Goose.* New York: HarperCollins, 2004.

Cusimano, MaryAnn K. *You Are My I Love You.* Illustrated by Satomi Ichikawa. New York: Philomel, 2001.

dePaola, Tomie, ed. *Tomie's Little Book of Poems.* New York: G. P. Putnam's Sons, 1988.

Dewdney, Anna. *Grumpy Gloria.* New York: Viking, 2006.

Eichenberg, Fritz. *Ape in a Cape: An Alphabet of Odd Animals.* New York: Harcourt, 1952.

Ets, Marie Hall. *In the Forest.* New York: Viking, 1944.

Ets, Marie Hall. *Play with Me.* New York: Puffin, 1976.

Feiffer, Jules. *The Daddy Mountain.* New York: Hyperion, 2004.

Fox, Mem. *The Magic Hat.* Illustrated by Tricia Tusa. New York: Harcourt, 2002.

Fox, Mem. *Shoes from Grandpa.* Illustrated by Patricia Mullins. New York: Orchard Books, 1989.

Fraser, Mary Ann. *How Animal Babies Stay Safe.* New York: HarperCollins, 2002.

Freeman, Don. *Quiet! There's a Canary in the Library.* New York: Penguin Young Readers, 2007.

Goennel, Heidi. *I Pretend.* New York: William Morrow, 1995.

Goodman, Joan Elizabeth. *Bernard's Bath.* Illustrated by Dominic Catalano. Honesdale, PA: Boyds Mills Press, 1996.

Greenfield, Eloise. *Honey, I Love.* Illustrated by Jan Spivey Gilchrest. New York: HarperCollins, 2003.

Gritz, Ona. *Tangerines and Tea: My Grandparents and Me.* Illustrated by Yumi Heo. New York: Harry N. Abrams, 2005.

Harper, Isabelle. *My Cats Nick and Nora.* Illustrated by Barry Moser. New York: Scholastic, 1995.

Harper, Isabelle. *My Dog Rosie.* Illustrated by Barry Moser. New York: Scholastic, 1994.

Harper, Jessica. *I'm Not Going to Chase the Cat Today!* Illustrated by Lindsay Harper DuPont. New York: HarperCollins, 2000.

Harper, Jessica. *Nora's Room.* Illustrated by Lindsay Harper DuPont. New York: HarperCollins, 2001.

Harshman, Marc. *Only One Neighborhood.* Illustrated by Barbara Garrison. New York: Dutton, 2007.

Henkes, Kevin. *Julius's Candy Corn.* New York: HarperCollins, 2003.

Henkes, Kevin. *Lilly's Chocolate Heart.* New York: HarperCollins, 2004.

Hoban, Russell. *Bread and Jam for Frances.* Illustrated by Lillian Hoban. New York: HarperTrophy, 1987.

Hoff, Sid. *Danny and the Dinosaur.* New York: HarperCollins, 1958.

Hutchins, Pat. *Don't Forget the Bacon.* New York: Mulberry, 1976.

Jackson, Louise, and Paul Harrison. *Guess What I'll Be.* Illustrated by Anni Axworthy. Cambridge, MA: Candlewick Press, 1998.

Jenkins, Steve, and Robin Page. *Move!* Illustrated by Steve Jenkins. New York: Houghton Mifflin, 2003.

Keller, Holly. *Help! A Story of Friendship.* New York: Greenwillow, 2007.

King, Stephen Michael. *Emily Loves to Bounce.* New York: Philomel, 2003.

Kraus, Robert. *Leo the Late Bloomer.* New York: Windmill Books, 1971.

Kraus, Robert. *Milton the Early Riser.* Illustrated by Jose Aruego and Ariane Dewey. New York: Aladdin, 1972.

Krauss, Ruth. *A Hole Is to Dig: A First Book of First Definitions.* Illustrated by Maurice Sendak. New York: Harper & Row, 1952.

Kroll, Virginia. *Busy, Busy Mouse.* Illustrated by Fumi Kosaka. New York: Viking, 2003.

Krull, Kathleen. *M Is for Music.* Illustrated by Stacy Innerst. New York: Harcourt, 2003.

Kulka, Joe. *Wolf's Coming*. Minneapolis, MN: Lerner/CarolRhoda Books, 2007.

Kuskin, Karla. *Roar and More*. New York: Harper & Row, 1956.

La Rochelle, David. *The Best Pet of All*. Illustrated by Hanako Wakiyama. New York: Dutton, 2004.

Lee, Hector Viveros. *I Had a Hippopotamus*. New York: Lee & Low Books, 1996.

Lionni, Leo. *A Color of His Own*. New York: Scholastic, 1975.

Lionni, Leo. *Swimmy*. New York: Scholastic, 1963.

Lobel, Anita. *Nini Here and There*. New York: Greenwillow, 2007.

Lobel, Arthur. *On Market Street*. Illustrated by Anita Lobel. New York: Greenwillow, 1981.

London, Jonathan. *My Big Rig*. Illustrated by Viviana Garofoli. Tarrytown, NY: Marshall Cavendish Children, 2007.

Loomis, Christine. *Rush Hour*. Illustrated by Mari Takabayashi. Boston: Houghton Mifflin, 1996.

Low, Alice. *Aunt Lucy Went to Buy a Hat*. Illustrated by Laura Huliska-Beith. New York: HarperCollins, 2004.

Martin, Bill Jr. *Panda Bear, Panda Bear, What Do You See?* Illustrated by Eric Carle. New York: Henry Holt, 2003.

Metropolitan Museum of Art. *Museum ABC*. New York: Little, Brown, 2002.

Modarressi, Mitra. *Stay Awake, Sally*. New York: G. P. Putnam's Sons, 2007.

Neubecker, Robert. *Wow! City!* New York: Hyperion, 2004.

Norworth, Jack. *Take Me Out to the Ballgame*. Illustrated by Maryann Kovalski. Toronto, Ontario: North Winds Press, 1992.

O'Connor, Jane. *Ready, Set, Skip!* Illustrated by Ann James. New York: Viking, 2007.

Ormerod, Jan. *Miss Mouse's Day*. New York: HarperCollins, 2001.

Otto, Carolyn. *Our Puppies Are Growing*. Illustrated by Mary Morgan. New York: HarperCollins, 1998.

Pallotta, Jerry. *The Icky Bug Alphabet Book*. Illustrated by Ralph Masiello. Watertown, MA: Charlesbridge, 1987. (See other alphabet books by this author.)

Paraskevas, Betty. *On the Edge of the Sea*. Illustrated by Michael Paraskevas. New York: Aladdin, 1992.

Paxton, Tom. *The Jungle Baseball Game*. Illustrated by Karen Lee Schmidt. New York: Morrow Junior Books, 1999.

Polacco, Patricia. *G Is for Goat*. New York: Philomel, 2003.

Portis, Antoinette. *Not a Box*. New York: HarperCollins, 2006.

Rockwell, Anne. *Bumblebee, Bumblebee, Do You Know Me?: A Garden Guessing Game*. New York: HarperCollins, 1999.

Rockwell, Anne. *My Pet Hamster*. Illustrated by Bernice Lum. New York: HarperCollins, 2002.

Russo, Marisabina. *The Big Brown Box*. New York: Greenwillow, 2000.

Ryan, Pam Muñoz. *Armadillos Sleep in Dugouts: and Other Places Animals Live*. Illustrated by Diane deGroat. New York: Hyperion, 1997.

Scanlon, Elizabeth Garton. *A Sock Is a Pocket for Your Toes: A Pocket Book*. Illustrated by Robin Preiss Glasser. New York: HarperCollins, 2004.

Schertle, Alice. *Teddy Bear, Teddy Bear: Poems by Alice Schertle*. Illustrated by Linda Hill Griffith. New York: HarperCollins, 2003.

Sendak, Maurice. *Alligators All Around: An Alphabet*. New York: HarperTrophy, 1962.

Sendak, Maurice. *Chicken Soup with Rice: A Book of Months*. New York: HarperTrophy, 1962.

Sendak, Maurice. *One Was Johnny: A Counting Book*. New York: HarperTrophy, 1962.

Sendak, Maurice. *Pierre: A Cautionary Tale in Five Chapters and a Prologue*. New York: HarperTrophy, 1962.

Shaw, Charles, G. *It Looked Like Spilt Milk*. New York: HarperCollins, 1947.

Shulman, Lisa. *Old MacDonald Had a Woodshop*. Illustrated by Ashley Wolff. New York: G. P. Putnam's Sons, 2002.

Stoeke, Janet Morgan. *Minerva Louise and the Red Truck*. New York: Dutton, 2002. (See other books in this series.)

Ungerer, Tomi. *Crictor*. New York: HarperTrophy, 1983.

Van Leeuwen, Jean. *Wait for Me! Said Maggie McGee*. Illustrated by Jacqueline Rogers. New York: Phyllis Fogelman Books, 2001.

Wallace, Karen. *Red Fox*. Illustrated by Peter Melnyczuk. Cambridge, MA: Candlewick Press, 1994.

Walsh, Ellen. *Mouse Paint*. New York: Harcourt, 1989.

Walton, Rick. *That's My Dog!* Illustrated by Julia Gorton. New York: G. P. Putnam's Sons, 2001.

Wells, Rosemary. *Bunny Cakes*. New York: Puffin, 2000.

Wells, Rosemary, illus. *Getting to Know You: Rodgers and Hammerstein Favorites*. New York: HarperCollins, 2002.

Wells, Rosemary. *Noisy Nora*. New York: Puffin, 2000.

Wilson, Karma. *A Frog in the Bog*. Illustrated by Joan Rankin. New York: Margaret McElderry Books, 2003.

Yee, Brenda Shannon. *Sand Castle*. Illustrated by Thea Kliros. New York: Greenwillow, 1999.

Yolen, Jane. *This Little Piggy and Other Rhymes to Sing and Play*. Illustrated by Will Hillenbrand. Cambridge, MA: Candlewick Press, 2005.

Zalben, Jane Breskin. *Hey, Mama Goose*. Illustrated by Emilie Chollat. New York: Dutton, 2005.

Zemach, Kaethe. *Just Enough and Not Too Much*. New York: Scholastic, 2003.

Ziefert, Harriet. *When I First Came to This Land*. Illustrated by Simms Taback. New York: G. P. Putnam's Sons, 1998.

Zolotow, Charlotte. *Some Things Go Together*. Illustrated by Karen Gundersheimer. New York: Thomas Y. Crowell, 1969.

# 4- to 5-Year-Olds

Aliki. *All by Myself!* New York: HarperCollins, 2000.

Arnosky, Jim. *Raccoon on His Own*. New York: G. P. Putnam's Sons, 2001.

Asch, Frank. *Moonbear's Dream*. New York: Aladdin, 1999.

Baker, Jeannie. *The Hidden Forest*. New York: Greenwillow, 2000.

Baker, Leslie. *The Third Story Cat*. Boston: Little, Brown, 1987.

Barrett, Judi. *Animals Should Definitely Not Wear Clothing*. Illustrated by Ron Barrett. New York: Aladdin, 1974.

Beaumont, Karen. *I Like Myself*. Illustrated by David Catrow. New York: Scholastic, 2004.

Bemelmans, Ludwig. *Madeline*. New York: Viking, 1939.

Bond, Rebecca. *This Place in the Snow*. New York: Dutton, 2004.

Booth, Philip. *Crossing*. Illustrated by Bagram Ibatoulline. Cambridge, MA: Candlewick Press, 2001.

Bradley, Kimberly Brubaker. *Pop! A Book About Bubbles*. Photographs by Margaret Miller. New York: HarperCollins, 2001.

Brooks, Alan. *Frogs Jump*. Illustrated by Steven Kellogg. New York: Scholastic, 1996.

Brown, Margaret Wise. *The Important Book*. Illustrated by Leonard Weisgard. New York: Harper & Row, 1949.

Bryan, Ashley, illus. *Let It Shine: Three Favorite Spirituals*. New York: Atheneum, 2007.

Burton, Virginia Lee. *Mike Mulligan and His Steam Shovel*. New York: Houghton Mifflin, 1939.

Carle, Eric, illus. *Eric Carle's Animals Animals* (poetry anthology). New York: Puffin, 1989.

Carle, Eric. *Mr. Seahorse*. New York: Philomel, 2004.

Charlip, Remy. *Fortunately*. New York: Macmillan, 1964.

Cohen, Caron Lee. *Where's the Fly?* New York: Greenwillow, 1996.

Coplans, Peta. *Cat and Dog*. New York: Viking, 1996.

Cronin, Doreen. *Click. Clack. Quackity-Quack: An Alphabetical Adventure*. Illustrated by Betsy Lewin. New York: Atheneum, 2005.

Cullinan, Bernice E., ed. *I Heard a Bluebird Sing: Children Select Their Favorite Poems by Aileen Fisher*. Illustrated by Jennifer Emery. Honesdale, PA; Boyds Mills Press, 2002.

de Brunhoff, Jean. *The Story of Babar, the Little Elephant*. New York: Random House, 1931.

dePaola, Tomie. *Strega Nona*. New York: Simon & Schuster, 1975.

Dewey, Jennifer Owings. *Faces Only a Mother Could Love*. Honesdale, PA: Boyds Mills Press, 1996.

Duffy, Dee Dee. *Forest Tracks*. Illustrated by Janet Marshall. Honesdale, PA: Boyds Mills Press, 1996.

Ehlert, Lois. *Hands: Growing Up to Be an Artist*. New York: Harcourt, 2004.

Ets, Marie Hall. *Gilberto and the Wind*. New York: Viking, 1963.

Farjeon, Eleanor. *Cats Sleep Anywhere*. Illustrated by Anne Mortimer. New York: HarperCollins, 1996.

Feelings, Muriel. *Jambo Means Hello: Swahili Alphabet Book*. Illustrated by Tom Feelings. New York: Puffin, 1992.

Feiffer, Jules. *Bark, George*. New York: HarperCollins, 1999.

Fox, Mem. *Night Noises*. Illustrated by Terry Denton. New York: Harcourt, 1989.

Fox, Mem. *Tough Boris*. Illustrated by Kathryn Brown. New York: Harcourt, 1994.

Gackenbach, Dick. *Supposes*. New York: Harcourt Brace Jovanovich, 1989.

George, Kristine O'Connell. *Little Dog Poems*. Illustrated by June Otani. New York: Clarion Books, 1999.

Geringer, Laura. *A Three Hat Day*. Illustrated by Arnold Lobel. New York: Harper & Row, 1985.

Gershator, Phillis. *When It Starts to Snow*. Illustrated by Martin Matje. New York: Henry Holt, 1998.

Greenfield, Eloise. *I Can Draw a Weeposaur and Other Dinosaurs*. Illustrated by Jan Spivey Gilchrest. New York: Greenwillow, 2001.

Grunwald, Lisa. *Now Soon Later*. Illustrated by Jane Johnson. New York: Greenwillow, 1996.

Hardendorff, Jeanne B. *The Bed Just So*. Illustrated by Lisl Weil. New York: Scholastic, 1975.

Harper, Jessica. *Lizzie's Do's and Don'ts*. Illustrated by Lindsay Harper du Pont. New York: HarperCollins, 2002.

Hoberman, Mary Ann. *The Cozy Book*. Illustrated by Betty Fraser. New York: Harcourt, 1980.

Hoberman, Mary Ann. *A Fine Fat Pig*. Illustrated by Malcah Zeldis. New York: HarperCollins, 1991.

Hoberman, Mary Ann. *A House Is a House for Me*. Illustrated by Betty Fraser. New York: Puffin Books, 1978.

Hoberman, Mary Ann. *The Llama Who Had No Pajama: 100 Favorite Poems by Mary Ann Hoberman*. Illustrated by Betty Fraser. New York: Harcourt, 1998.

Hopkins, Lee Bennett, ed. *Still as a Star: A Book of Nighttime Poems*. Illustrated by Karen Milone. New York: Little, Brown, 1989.

Hutchins, Pat. *Shrinking Mouse*. New York: Greenwillow, 1997.

Joyce, William. *George Shrinks*. New York: Harper & Row, 1985.

Keats, Ezra Jack. *Jennie's Hat*. New York: HarperTrophy, 1966.

Keats, Ezra Jack. *The Snowy Day*. New York: Penguin Books, 1962.

Keats, Ezra Jack. *Whistle for Willie*. New York: Viking, 1964.

Kellogg, Steven. *Can I Keep Him?* New York: Dial Books for Young Readers, 1971.

Kellogg, Steven. *Won't Somebody Play with Me?* New York: Dial Books for Young Readers, 1971.

Kvasnosky, Laura McGee. *See You Later, Alligator!* San Diego: Harcourt, 1995.

Leaf, Munro. *The Story of Ferdinand*. Illustrated by Robert Lawson. New York: Viking, 1936.

Lember, Barbara Hirsch. *The Shell Book*. Boston: Houghton Mifflin, 1997.

Lionni, Leo. *Alexander and the Wind-Up Mouse*. New York: Pantheon, 1969.

Lionni, Leo. *Inch by Inch*. New York: Scholastic, 1960.

Lobel, Arnold. *Frog and Toad Are Friends*. New York: Harper & Row, 1970.

Manushkin, Fran. *Baby, Come Out*. Illustrated by Ronald Himler. New York: HarperTrophy, 1972.

Markes, Julie. *Shhhh! Everybody's Sleeping*. Illustrated by David Parkin. New York: HarperCollins, 2005.

Martin, Mary Jane. *From Anne to Zach*. Illustrated by Michael Grejniec. Honesdale, PA: Boyds Mills Press, 1996.

Mayer, Mercer. *The Bravest Knight*. New York: Dial, 2007.

Mayer, Mercer. *What Do You Do with a Kangaroo?* New York: Scholastic, 1973.

Moore, Lilian. *Little Raccoon and the Outside World*. Illustrated by Gioia Fiammenghi. New York: Scholastic, 1965.

Neubecker, Robert. *Wow! America!* New York: Hyperion, 2006.

Numeroff, Laura Joffe. *Chimps Don't Wear Glasses*. Illustrated by Joe Mathieu. New York: Simon & Schuster, 1995.

Numeroff, Laura Joffe. *Dogs Don't Wear Sneakers*. Illustrated by Joe Mathieu. New York: Simon & Schuster, 1993.

Numeroff, Laura Joffe, *If You Give a Mouse a Cookie*. Illustrated by Felicia Bond. New York: HarperCollins, 2000. (See other books in this series.)

Pallotta, Jerry. *The Construction Alphabet Book*. Illustrated by Rob Bolster. Watertown, MA: Charlesbridge, 2006. (See many other alphabet books by this author.)

Paxton, Tom. *The Marvelous Toy*. Illustrated by Elizabeth Sayles. New York: Morrow, 1996.

Piven, Hanoch. *The Perfect Purple Feather*. New York: HarperCollins, 1985.

Polacco, Patricia. *Emma Kate*. New York: Philomel, 2005.

Roberts, Bethany, and Patricia Hubbell. *Camel Caravan*. Illustrated by Cheryl Munro Taylor. New York: Tambourine, 1996.

Rogers, Paul, and Emma Rogers. *Quacky Duck*. Illustrated by B. Mullarney Wright. Boston: Little, Brown, 1995.

Roth, Susan. *My Love for You*. New York: Dial, 1997.

Russo, Marisabina. *Under the Table*. New York: Greenwillow, 1997.

Schaefer, Lola. *This Is the Rain*. Illustrated by Jane Wattenberg. New York: Greenwillow, 2001.

Sendak, Maurice. *Where the Wild Things Are*. New York: Harper & Row, 1963.

Shulevitz, Uri. *Rain Rain Rivers*. New York: Farrar, Straus and Giroux, 1969.

Simmons, Jane. *Ebb and Flo and the New Friend*. New York: Orchard Children's Books, 1998.

Simon, Norma. *Wet World*. Illustrated by Alexi Natchev. Cambridge, MA: Candlewick Press, 1995.

Slepian, Jan, and Ann Seidler. *The Hungry Thing*. Illustrated by Richard E. Martin. New York: Scholastic, 1967.

Spilka, Arnold. *Monkeys Write Terrible Letters and Other Poems*. Honesdale, PA: Boyds Mills Press, 1994.

Spinelli, Eileen. *I Know It's Autumn*. Illustrated by Nancy Hayashi. New York: HarperCollins, 2004.

Stringer, Lauren. *Winter Is the Warmest Season*. New York: Harcourt, 2006.

Tafuri, Nancy. *The Brass Ring*. New York: Greenwillow, 1996.

Van Rynbach, Iris. *Five Little Pumpkins*. Honesdale, PA: Boyds Mills Press, 1995.

Walsh, Jill Paton. *Connie Came to Play*. Illustrated by Stephen Lambert. New York: Viking, 1995.

Watson, Clyde. *Father Fox's Penny Rhymes*. Illustrated by Wendy Watson. New York: Thomas Y. Crowell, 1971.

Williams, Barbara. *If He's My Brother*. Illustrated by Tomie dePaola. Englewood Cliffs, NJ: Prentice-Hall, 1976.

Yarrow, Peter, and Lenny Lipton. *Puff the Magic Dragon*. Illustrated by Eric Puybaret. New York: Sterling, 2007.

Yashima, Taro. *Umbrella*. New York: Puffin, 1958.

Yolen, Jane. *The Three Bears Rhyme Book*. Illustrated by Jane Dyer. New York: Harcourt Brace Jovanovich, 1987.

Young, Dianne. *Purple Hair? I Don't Care!* Illustrated by Barbara Hartmann. Brooklyn, NY: Kane/Miller, 1995.

Ziefert, Harriet. *39 Uses for a Friend*. Illustrated by Rebecca Doughty. New York: G. P. Putnam's Sons, 2001.

Zion, Gene. *Harry the Dirty Dog*. Illustrated by Margaret Bloy Graham. New York: Harper & Row, 1956.

Zolotow, Charlotte. *When the Wind Stops*. Illustrated by Stefano Vitale. New York: HarperCollins, 1962.

Zolotow, Charlotte. *William's Doll*. Illustrated by William Pene du Bois. New York: HarperCollins, 1972.

## 5- to 6-Year-Olds

Ahlberg, Janet, and Allan Ahlberg. *The Jolly Postman or Other People's Letters*. New York: Little, Brown, 1986.

Barrett, Judi. *Cloudy with a Chance of Meatballs*. Illustrated by Ron Barrett. New York: Atheneum, 1978.

Barrett, Judi. *Things That Are the Most in the World*. Illustrated by John Nickle. New York: Aladdin, 2001.

Bate, Lucy. *Little Rabbit's Loose Tooth*. Illustrated by Diane DeGroat. New York: Scholastic, 1975.

Berger, Barbara Helen. *A Lot of Otters*. New York: Philomel, 1997.

Bloom, Suzanne. *A Splendid Friend Indeed*. Honesdale, PA: Boyds Mills Press, 2005.

Bottner, Barbara, and George Kruglik. *Wallace's Lists*. Illustrated by Olof Landstrom. New York: HarperCollins, 2004.

Brett, Jan. *The Three Snow Bears*. New York: Putnam, 2007.

Broach, Elise. *Wet Dog!* Illustrated by David Catrow. New York: Dial Books for Young Readers, 2005.

Browne, Anthony. *Shape Game.* New York: Farrar, Straus and Giroux, 2002.

Browne, Anthony. *Through the Magic Mirror.* New York: Walker Books, 2001.

Cazet, Denys. *Will You Read to Me?* New York: Atheneum, 2007.

Child, Lauren. *Clarice Bean, That's Me.* Cambridge, MA: Candlewick Press, 1999.

Child, Lauren. *I Will Never Not Ever Eat a Tomato.* Cambridge, MA: Candlewick Press, 2000. (See other Charlie and Lola books in this series.)

Chodos, Irvine Margaret. *Ellah Sarah Gets Dressed.* New York: Harcourt, 2003.

Clements, Andrew. *Workshop.* Illustrated by David Wisniewski. New York: Clarion, 1999.

Cole, Joanna. *The Magic School Bus: Inside a Beehive.* Illustrated by Bruce Degen. New York: Scholastic, 1996. (See other books in this nonfiction series.)

Crews, Donald. *Big Mama's.* New York: Greenwillow, 1991.

Cronin, Doreen. *Click, Clack, Moo: Cows That Type.* Illustrated by Betsy Lewin. New York: Simon & Schuster, 2000.

Curtis, Jamie Lee. *I'm Gonna Like Me: Letting Off a Little Self-Esteem.* Illustrated by Laura Cornell. New York: HarperCollins, 2002.

Curtis, Jamie Lee. *It's Hard to Be Five: Learning How to Work My Control Panel.* Illustrated by Laura Cornell. New York: HarperCollins, 2004.

Cuyler, Margery. *100th Day Worries.* Illustrated by Arthur Howard. New York: Simon & Schuster, 2000.

de Regniers, Beatrice Schenk et al. (eds.). *Sing a Song of Popcorn: Every Child's Book of Poems.* Illustrated by Marcia Brown et al. New York: Scholastic, 1988.

Dr. Seuss. *Horton Hatches the Egg.* New York: Random House, 1940.

Duvoisin, Roger. *Petunia.* New York: Alfred A. Knopf, 1950.

Edwards, Pamela Duncan. *The Old House.* Illustrated by Henry Cole. New York: Dutton, 2007.

Franco, Betsy. *Birdsongs.* Illustrated by Steve Jenkins. New York: Margaret K. McElderry Books, 2007.

Frasier, Debra. *Out of the Ocean.* New York: Harcourt, 1998.

Gilman, Phoebe. *Something from Nothing.* New York: Scholastic, 1992.

Gravett, Emily. *Wolves.* New York: Simon & Schuster, 2005.

Greenfield, Eloise. *Me & Neesie.* Illustrated by Moneta Barnett. New York: Harper & Row, 1975.

Halpern, Sheri. *What Shall We Do When We All Go Out?* New York: North South, 1995.

Harper, Jessica. *A Place Called Kindergarten.* Illustrated by G. Brian Karas. New York: G. P. Putnam's Sons, 2006.

Henkes, Kevin. *Wemberley Worried.* New York: Greenwillow, 2003.

Hennessy, B. G. *Mr. Ouchy's First Day.* Illustrated by Paul Meisel. New York: G. P. Putnam's Sons, 2006.

Hoberman, Mary Ann. *The Seven Silly Eaters.* Illustrated by Marla Frazee. New York: Harcourt, 1997.

Hoberman, Mary Ann. *You Read to Me, I'll Read to You: Very Short Scary Tales to Read Together.* Illustrated by Michael Emberley. New York: Little, Brown, 2007.

Hofsepian, Sylvia. *Why Not?* Illustrated by Friso Henstra. New York: Macmillan, 1991.

Holabird, Katharine. *Alexander and the Dragon.* Illustrated by Helen Craig. New York: Clarkson N. Potter, 1988.

Howard, Arthur. *When I Was Five.* San Diego: Harcourt, 1996.

Howe, James. *Horace and Morris but Mostly Dolores.* Illustrated by Amy Walrod. New York: Atheneum, 1999.

Howe, James. *There's a Monster Under My Bed.* Illustrated by David Rose. New York: Atheneum, 1986.

Hutchens, Hazel. *A Second Is a Hiccup: A Child's Book of Time.* Illustrated by Kady MacDonald Denton. New York: Arthur A. Levine Books, 2007.

Isadora, Rachel. *What a Family! A Fresh Look at Family Trees.* New York: G. P. Putnam's Sons, 2007.

James, Simon. *Leon and Bob.* Cambridge, MA: Candlewick Press, 1997.

James, Simon. *The Wild Woods.* Cambridge, MA: Candlewick Press, 1993.

Jenkins, Steve, and Robin Page. *What Do You Do with a Tail Like This?* New York: Houghton Mifflin, 2003.

Jones, Rebecca C. *Great Aunt Martha.* Illustrated by Shelley Jackson. New York: Dutton, 1995.

Juster, Norton. *The Hello, Goodbye Window.* Illustrated by Chris Raschka. New York: Hyperion, 2005.

Katz, Bobbi, ed. *Pocket Poems.* Illustrated by Marilyn Hafner. New York: Dutton, 2004.

Knudsen, Michelle. *Library Lion.* Illustrated by Kevin Hawkes. Cambridge, MA: Candlewick Press, 2006.

Komaiko, Leah. *I Like the Music.* Illustrated by Barbara Westman. New York: HarperTrophy, 1987.

Kuskin, Karla. *The Dallas Titans Get Ready for Bed.* Illustrations by Marc Simont. New York: Harper & Row, 1986.

Kuskin, Karla. *Moon, Have You Met My Mother? The Collected Poems of Karla Kuskin.* Illustrated by Sergio Ruzzier. New York: HarperCollins, 2003.

Kuskin, Karla. *The Philharmonic Gets Dressed.* Illustrations by Marc Simont. New York: HarperTrophy, 1982.

Lendler, Ian. *An Undone Fairy Tale.* Illustrated by Whitney Martin. New York: Simon & Schuster, 2005.

Lester, Helen. *It Wasn't My Fault.* Illustrated by Lynn Munsinger. New York: Houghton Mifflin, 1985.

Lester, Helen. *A Porcupine Named Fluffy.* Illustrated by Lynn Munsinger. New York: Houghton Mifflin, 1986.

Lowery, Linda. *Twist with a Burger, Jitter with a Bug.* Illustrated by Pat Dypold. Boston: Houghton Mifflin, 1995.

Margolis, Richard J. *Secrets of a Small Brother.* Illustrated by Donald Carrick. New York: Macmillan, 1984.

Markle, Sandra. *Outside and Inside Dinosaurs.* New York: Atheneum, 2000. (See other nonfiction books in this series.)

Marshall, James. *George and Martha.* New York: Scholastic, 1972.

Mayer, Mercer. *There Are Monsters Everywhere.* New York: Dial, 2005.

McCaughrean, Geraldine. *My Grandfather's Clock.* New York: Clarion, 2002.

McCloskey, Robert. *Blueberries for Sal.* New York: Viking, 1948.

McCloskey, Robert. *Make Way for Ducklings.* New York: Viking, 1941.

McNulty, Faith. *If You Decide to Go to the Moon.* Illustrated by Steven Kellogg. New York: Scholastic, 2005.

McPhail, David. *Sisters.* New York: Harcourt, 2003.

Meisel, Paul. *Zara's Hats.* New York: Puffin Books, 2003.

Moss, Lloyd. *Zin! Zin! Zin! A Violin.* Illustrated by Marjorie Priceman. New York: Aladdin, 1995.

Munsch, Robert. *The Paper Bag Princess.* Illustrated by Michael Martchenko. Vancouver, BC: Annick Press, 1980.

Naylor, Phyllis Reynolds. *King of the Playground.* Illustrated by Nola Langner Malone. New York: Aladdin, 1991.

Noble, Trinka Hakes. *The Day Jimmy's Boa Ate the Wash.* Illustrated by Steven Kellogg. New York: Dial Books for Young Readers, 1980.

Offill, Jenny. *17 Things I'm Not Allowed to Do Anymore.* Illustrated by Nancy Carpenter. New York: Schwartz & Wade Books, 2007.

O'Neill, Alexis. *The Recess Queen.* Illustrated by Laura Huliska-Beith. New York: Scholastic, 2002.

Owens, Mary Beth. *Panda Whispers.* New York: Dutton, 2007.

Palatini, Margie. *The Perfect Pet.* Illustrated by Bruce Whatley. New York: HarperCollins, 2003.

Parr, Todd. *Reading Makes You Feel Good.* New York: Little, Brown, 2005.

Pilkey, Dav. *The Paperboy.* New York: Orchard, 1996.

Rathmann, Peggy. *Bootsie Barker Bites.* New York: Scholastic, 1992.

Rathmann, Peggy. *Ruby the Copycat.* New York: Scholastic, 1991.

Reynolds, Peter H. *The Dot.* Cambridge, MA: Candlewick Press, 2003.

Ridlon, Marci. *Sun Through the Window: Poems for Children.* Honesdale, PA: Boyds Mills Press, 1996.

Robertson, M. P. *The Egg.* New York: Puffin, 2000.

Roth, Susan L. *Great Big Guinea Pigs.* London: Bloomsbury Children's Books, 2006.

Rylant, Cynthia. *In November.* Illustrated by Jill Kastner. New York: Harcourt, 2000.

Schachner, Judy. *Skippyjon Jones.* New York: Dutton, 2003.

Schwartz, Amy. *Annabelle Swift, Kindergartner.* New York: Scholastic, 1991.

Sharmat, Marjorie Weinman. *Gila Monsters Meet You at the Airport*. Illustrated by Byron Barton. New York: Puffin Books, 1980.

Shields, Carol Diggory. *Lucky Pennies and Hot Chocolate*. Illustrated by Hiroe Nakata. New York: Puffin Books, 2002.

Siddals, Mary McKenna. *Tell Me a Season*. New York: Clarion, 1997.

Sierra, Judy. *Wild About Books*. New York: Knopf, 2004.

Slepian, Jan. *Emily Just in Time*. New York: Philomel, 1998.

Spinelli, Eileen. *Do You Have a Hat?* New York: Simon & Schuster, 2004.

Spinelli, Eileen. *Somebody Loves You, Mr. Hatch*. New York: Aladdin, 1991.

Steig, William. *Doctor DeSoto*. New York: Farrar, Straus and Giroux, 1982.

Steig, William. *Sylvester and the Magic Pebble*. New York: Simon & Schuster, 1969.

Swift, Hildegarde H., and Lynd Ward. *The Little Red Lighthouse and the Great Gray Bridge*. New York: Harcourt, 1942.

Taylor, Mark. *The Frog House*. Illustrated by Barbara Garrison. New York: Dutton, 2004.

Thomas, Shelley Moore. *Take Care, Good Knight*. Illustrated by Paul Meisel. New York: Dutton, 2006.

Viorst, Judith. *I'll Fix Anthony*. Illustrated by Arnold Lobel. New York: Harper & Row, 1969.

Waber, Bernard. *Ira Sleeps Over*. New York: Houghton Mifflin, 1972.

Waber, Bernard. *Lyle, Lyle, Crocodile*. New York: Houghton Mifflin, 1965.

Waite, Judy. *Mouse, Look Out!* Illustrated by Norma Burgin. New York: Dutton, 1998.

Walsh, Jill Paton. *When I Was Little like You*. Illustrated by Stephen Lambert. New York: Penguin, 1997.

Willans, Tom. *Wait! I Want to Tell You a Story*. New York: Simon & Schuster, 2004.

Willey, Margaret. *Clever Beatrice*. Illustrated by Heather M. Solomon. New York: Aladdin, 2001.

Williams, Vera B. *A Chair for My Mother*. New York: Greenwillow, 1982.

Wood, Audrey. *Rude Giants*. New York: Harcourt, 1993.

Zolotow, Charlotte. *I Like to Be Little*. Illustrated by Erik Blegvad. New York: HarperTrophy, 1966.

Zolotow, Charlotte. *If It Weren't for You*. Illustrated by G. Brian Karas. New York: HarperCollins, 1994.

# Must-Know Nonfiction Writers for Children Ages 2 to 6

David Adler
Aliki
George Ancona
Jim Arnosky
Byron Barton
Melvin Berger
Louise Borden
Franklyln Branley
Vicki Cobb
Joanna Cole
Jennifer Owings Dewey

Leonard Everett Fisher
Russell Freedman
Jean Fritz
Jean Craighead George
Gail Gibbons
Augusta Goldin
Tana Hoban
Steve Jenkins
Jill Krementz
Patricia Lauber
David Macaulay

Betsy Maestro
Mick Manning
Sandra Markle
Roxie Munro
Ann Morris
Wendy Pfeffer
Laurence Pringle
Ken Robbins
Anne Rockwell
Pam Muñoz Ryan
Lola Schaefer

Millicent Selsam
Paul Showers
Seymour Simon
Marilyn Singer
Peter Sis
Diane Stanley
Anastasia Suen
Karen Wallace

# Must-Know Poets for Children Ages 2 to 6

Arnold Adoff
Dorothy Aldis
Margaret Wise Brown
John Ciardi
Lucille Clifton
William Cole
Beatrice Schenk deRegniers
Rebecca Kai Dotlich
Barbara Esbensen
Eleanor Farjeon
Aileen Fisher
Douglas Florian

Kristine O'Connell George
Nikki Giovanni
Eloise Greenfield
Monica Gunning
Mary Ann Hoberman
Lee Bennett Hopkins
Langston Hughes
Bobbi Katz
X. J. Kennedy
Karla Kuskin
Edward Lear
Dennis Lee

Constance Levy
J. Patrick Lewis
Myra Cohn Livingston
Richard Margolis
David McCord
Eve Merriam
A. A. Milne
Lilian Moore
Lillian Morrison
Mother Goose
Jack Prelutsky
Marci Ridlon

Christina Rossetti
Alice Schertle
Shel Silverstein
Arnold Spilka
Ann Turner
Valerie Worth

# Classic Stories to Share

Many versions of these classic stories are available in picture book format. Don't hesitate to share several retellings of each story.

## Aesop's Fables

*The Boy Who Cried Wolf*

*The Fox and the Grapes*

*The Goose That Laid the Golden Eggs*

*The Lion and the Mouse*

*The Miller, His Son and Their Donkey*

*The Tortoise and the Hare*

*The Town Mouse and the Country Mouse*

## Hans Christian Andersen

*The Emperor's New Clothes*

*The Little Match Girl*

*The Little Mermaid*

*The Princess and the Pea*

*Thumbelina*

*The Ugly Duckling*

## The Brothers Grimm

*The Bremen Town Musicians*

*Cinderella*

*The Elves and the Shoemaker*

*The Frog Prince*

*Hansel and Gretel*

*Little Red Hiding Hood*

*Rapunzel*

*Rumpelstiltskin*

*Sleeping Beauty*

*Snow White*

*Tom Thumb*

*Twelve Dancing Princesses*

## Rudyard Kipling's "Just So" Stories

*How the Camel Got His Hump*

*How the Elephant Got His Trunk*

*How the Leopard Got His Spots*

## A. A. Milne

*The House at Pooh Corner*

*Now We Are Six*

*When We Were Very Young*

*Winnie-the-Pooh*

## Beatrix Potter's Peter Rabbit Tales

*The Tale of Benjamin Bunny*

*The Tale of the Flopsy Bunnies*

*The Tale of Jemima Puddle-Duck*

*The Tale of Jeremy Fisher*

*The Tale of Mrs. Tiggy-Winkle*

*The Tale of Mrs. Tittlemouse*

*The Tale of Peter Rabbit*

*The Tale of Squirrel Nutkin*

*The Tale of Tom Kitten*

## Carl Sandburg's Rootabaga Stories

*The Story of Jason Squiff and Why He Had a Popcorn Hat, Popcorn Mittens and Popcorn Shoes*

*Three Boys With Jugs of Molasses and Secret Ambitions*

*The Wedding Procession of the Rag Doll and the Broom Handle and Who Was in It*

## Additional Classic Folk and Fairy Tales Too Good to Miss

After reading these traditional tales and their many versions, read the many takeoffs on these classic tales.

*Alice in Wonderland*

*Beauty and the Beast*

*The Brave Little Tailor*

*The Gingerbread Boy*

*Goldilocks and the Three Bears*

*Henny Penny*

*Jack and the Beanstalk*

*The Little Red Hen*

*Pinocchio*

*Puss in Boots*

*Stone Soup*

*The Three Billy Goats Gruff*

*The Three Little Pigs*

*The Three Sillies*

*The Three Wishes*

# Works Cited

**Activity #1: The Read-Aloud, Of Course**
*Good Thing You're Not an Octopus!* by Julie Markes

**Activity #2: Follow Their Lead**
*1-2-3: A Child's First Counting Book* by Alison Jay
*And the Dish Ran Away With the Spoon* by Janet Stevens and Susan Stevens Crummel
*Each Peach Pear Plum* by Janet Ahlberg and Allan Ahlberg
*The Fairy Tale Cake* by Mark Sperring
*Hey, Mama Goose* by Jane Breskin Zalben
*The Jolly Postman or Other People's Letters* by Janet Ahlberg and Allan Ahlberg
*Wait for Me! Said Maggie McGee* by Jean Van Leeuwen

**Activity #3: Illustration Peek-a-Boo**
*1-2-3: A Child's First Counting Book* by Alison Jay
*ABC: A Child's First Alphabet Book* by Alison Jay
*Dinosaur Train* by John Steven Gurney
*How Do Dinosaurs Clean their Rooms?* by Jane Yolen
*How Do Dinosaurs Count to Ten?* by Jane Yolen
*How Do Dinosaurs Eat Their Food?* by Jane Yolen
*How Do Dinosaurs Get Well Soon?* by Jane Yolen
*How Do Dinosaurs Go to School?* by Jane Yolen
*How Do Dinosaurs Play With Their Friends?* by Jane Yolen
*How Do Dinosaurs Say Goodnight?* by Jane Yolen
*Piggies* by Don Wood and Audrey Wood
*Tumble Bumble* by Felicia Bond

**Activity #4: Finding Five**
*Good Morning, Digger* by Anne Rockwell
*I Love Trucks* by Philemon Sturges
*My First Truck Board Book* by Dorling Kindersley
*Trucks* by Byron Barton
*Trucks Roll!* by George Ella Lyon
*Trucks, Trucks, Trucks* by Peter Sis
*Richard Scarry's Cars and Trucks and Things That Go* by Richard Scarry
*Seymour Simon's Book of Trucks* by Seymour Simon

**Activity #5: Rhyming Read-Alouds**
*Bunnies on the Go: Getting From Place to Place* by Rick Walton

**Activity #6: Hide-and-Seek With Books**
*Big Fish Little Fish* by Ed Heck
*Big Little* by Leslie Patricelli

*Over Under* by Marthe Jocelyn
*Quiet Loud* by Leslie Patricelli
*Yummy Yucky* by Leslie Patricelli

**Activity #7: Book Path Journey**
*Caps for Sale: A Tale of a Peddler, Some Monkeys and Their Monkey Business* by Esphyr Slobodkina
*Corduroy* by Don Freeman
*Where Is the Green Sheep?* by Mem Fox

**Activity #8: Board Book Building**
*The Carrot Seed* by Ruth Krauss
*Good Night, Gorilla* by Peggy Rathmann
*Goodnight Moon* by Margaret Wise Brown
*The Very Hungry Caterpillar* by Eric Carle

**Activity #9: Familiar Phrases**
*The Little Engine That Could* by Watty Piper

**Activity #10: Can't Stump Me**
*Caps for Sale* by Esphyr Slobodkina
*Once Upon a Time, the End (Asleep in 60 Seconds)* by Geoffrey Kloske

**Activity #11: Party Favor Storytelling**
Angelina Ballerina books by Katharine Holabird
Arthur books by Marc Brown
Bear books by Karma Wilson
Clifford books by Norman Bridwell
Curious George books by H. A. Rey and Margret Rey
Froggy books by Jonathan London
Jesse Bear books by Nancy White Carlstrom
Little Quack books by Lauren Thompson
Max and Ruby books by Rosemary Wells
Minerva Louise books by Janet Morgan Stoeke
Mouse's First . . . books by Lauren Thompson
Olivia books by Ian Falconer
Spot books by Eric Hill
Wibbly Pig books by Mick Inkpen

**Activity #12: Silly Story Fill-Ins**
*The Carrot Seed* by Ruth Krauss

**Activity #13: Toys and Texts**
*Angelina Ballerina* by Katharine Holabird
*Corduroy* by Don Freeman

*Curious George* by H. A. Rey

*Firefighter Frank* by Monica Wellington

*Goodnight Moon* by Margaret Wise Brown

*Harry the Dirty Dog* by Gene Zion

*I Like It When . . .* by Mary Murphy

*Leo the Late Bloomer* by Robert Krauss

*Maisy Takes a Bath* by Lucy Cousins

*Spot's Treasure Hunt* by Eric Hill

*The Story of Babar the Little Elephant* by Jean de Brunhoff

*Where Is the Green Sheep?* by Mem Fox

*Winnie-the-Pooh* by A. A. Milne

**Activity #14: Reading Faces, Reading Books**

*Alexander and the Terrible, Horrible, No Good, Very Bad Day* by Judith Viorst

*Pete's a Pizza* by William Steig

*Walter Was Worried* by Laura Vaccaro Seeger

*What Do You Do When a Monster Says Boo?* by Hope Vestergaard

*When Sophie Gets Angry . . . Really, Really Angry* by Molly Bang

**Activity #15: Between the Lines**

*Be Brown* by Barbara Bottner

*A Frog in the Bog* by Karma Wilson

*Going Up: A Color Counting Book* by Peter Sis

*Good Night, Gorilla* by Peggy Rathmann

*I'm Taking a Trip on My Train* by Shirley Nietzel

*Just Like Everyone Else* by Karla Kuskin

*Leon and Bob* by Simon James

*Little Dog Poems* by Kristine O'Connell George

*Never Give a Fish an Umbrella and Other Silly Presents* by Mike Thaler

*Nobody is Perfick* by Bernard Waber

*Way Down Deep in the Deep Blue Sea* by Jan Peck

*Way Far Away on a Wild Safari* by Jan Peck

*Way Up High in a Tall Green Tree* by Jan Peck

*Workshop* by Andrew Clements

**Activity #16: Questions Galore**

*Do Kangaroos Wear Seatbelts?* by Jane Kurtz

*"Hi, Pizza Man!"* by Virginia Walter

*It's Bedtime, Wibbly Pig!* by Mick Inkpen

*Owly* by Mike Thaler

*When Winter Comes* by Nancy Van Laan

*Where, Where Is Swamp Bear?* by Kathi Appelt

*Why Do Kittens Purr?* by Marion Dane Bauer

*Why Is the Sky Blue?* by Sally Grindley

*Would You Rather . . .* by John Burningham

**Activity #19: Bath-Time Rhymes**

*My Aunt Came Back* by Pat Cummings

**Activity #20: Mealtime Rhymes**

*I Scream, You Scream: A Feast of Food Rhymes* by Lillian Morrison

*Hot Potato: Mealtime Rhymes* by Neil Philip

*Tea Party Today: Poems to Sip and Savor* by Eileen Spinelli

*Yummy! Eating Through a Day* by Lee Bennett Hopkins (ed.)

**Activity #23: Alphabet Play**

*Alphabet City* by Stephen T. Johnson

**Activity #24: A Is for Apple**

*ABC Pop!* by Rachel Isadora

*Animal Alphabet* by Margriet Ruurs

*Appaloosa Zebra: A Horse Lover's Alphabet* by Jessie Haas

*Ellsworth's Extraordinary Electric Ears* by Valorie Fisher

**Activity #26: Songs to Draw**

*A Child's Book of Lullabies* by Shona McKellar

*Go In and Out the Window: An Illustrated Songbook for Young People* by Dan Fox

**Activity #28: Songs and Rhymes Personalized**

*My Aunt Came Back* by Pat Cummings

**Activity #29: Old Songs, New Versions**

*I Ain't Gonna Paint No More!* by Karen Beaumont

*I Know an Old Lady Who Swallowed a Pie* by Alison Jackson

*Old MacDonald Had a Woodshop* by Lisa Shulman

**Activity #30: Neighborhood Tours**

*Beachcombing: Exploring the Seashore* by Jim Arnosky

*Bugs, Bugs, Bugs* by Bob Barner

*Dog* by Matthew Van Fleet

*Take a Tree Walk* by Jane Kirkland

*The Wonder Book of Flowers* by Cynthia Iliff Koehler

**Activity #31: New Words Naturally**

*Bear Snores On* by Karma Wilson

*A Crowd of Cows* by John Graham

*Fancy Nancy* by Jane O'Connor

*Fancy Nancy and the Posh Puppy* by Jane O'Connor

*Kangaroos Have Joeys* by Philippa-Alys Browne

*The Napping House* by Audrey Wood

*A Pinky Is a Baby Mouse and Other Baby Animal Names* by Pam Muñoz Ryan

*Polar Bear, Polar Bear, What Do You Hear?* by Bill Martin, Jr., and Eric Carle

*Rain Romp: Stomping Away a Grouchy Day* by Jane Kurtz

*"Slowly, Slowly, Slowly," Said the Sloth* by Eric Carle

*Wild Birds* by Joanne Ryder

**Activity #33: Title Word Count**

*Caps for Sale* by Esphyr Slobodkina

*Chicka Chicka Boom Boom* by Bill Martin, Jr., and John Archambault

*The Daddy Book* by Ann Morris

*Jamberry* by Bruce Degen

*Knuffle Bunny: A Cautionary Tale* by Mo Willems

*Little Red Monkey* by Jonathan London

*Llama, Llama, Red Pajama* by Anna Dewdney

*Mr. Cookie Baker* by Monica Wellington

*Olivia* by Ian Falconer

*Pete's a Pizza* by William Steig

*Please, Baby, Please* by Spike Lee and Tonya Lewis Lee

*Sheep in a Jeep* by Nancy Shaw

*Snowmen at Night* by Caralyn Buehner

*Tanka, Tanka, Skunk!* by Steve Webb

*The Very Hungry Caterpillar* by Eric Carle

**Activity #37: Sign Search**

*City Signs* by Zoran Milich

*I See a Signs* by Lars Klove

*Mr. Pine's Mixed-Up Signs* by Leonard Kessler

*Once Upon a Banana* by Jennifer Armstrong

*Red, Yellow, Green: What Do Signs Mean?* by Joan Holub

*The Signmaker's Assistant* by Tedd Arnold

**Activity #41: Food Festivities**

*Apple Farmer Annie* by Monica Wellington

*Bee-Bim Bop* by Linda Sue Park

*The Bye-Bye Pie* by Sharon Jennings

*A Cake All for Me!* by Karen Magnuson Beil

*Carrot Soup* by John Segal

*Cook-a-Doodle-Doo!* by Janet Stevens and Susan Stevens Crummel

*The Cookie-Store Cat* by Cynthia Rylant

*A Day With My Aunts/Un dia con mis tias* by Anilú Bernardo

*Jingle Dancer* by Cynthia Leitich Smith

*The Moon Might Be Milk* by Lisa Shulman

*Mr. Cookie Baker* by Monica Wellington

*Pizza at Sally's* by Monica Wellington

**Activity #42: Language Delights**

*31 Uses for a Mom* by Harriet Ziefert

*40 Uses for a Grandpa* by Harriet Ziefert

*Amelia Bedelia* by Peggy Parrish

*As Silly as Knees, As Busy As Bees: An Astounding Assortment of Similes* by Norton Juster

*Busy Buzzing Bumblebees and Other Tongue Twisters* by Alvin Schwartz

*A Chocolate Moose for Dinner* by Fred Gwynne

*Cook-a-Doodle-Doo!* by Janet Stevens and Susan Stevens Crummel

*Did You Say Pears?* by Arlene Alda

*Don't Forget the Bacon* by Pat Hutchins

*Fishing in the Air* by Susan Creech

*Henry! The Dog with No Tail* by Kate Feiffer

*Hey, Hay! A Wagonful of Funny Homonym Riddles* by Marvin Terban

*A Honey of a Day* by Janet Marshall

*A Huge Hog Is a Big Pig: A Rhyming Word Game* by Francis McCall and Patricia Keeler

*I Love You as Much . . .* by Laura Krauss Melmed

*Incredible Me!* by Kathi Appelt

*The King Who Rained* by Fred Gwynne

*Knock, Knock!* by Saxton Freymann

*A Little Pigeon Toad* by Fred Gwynne

*My Teacher Likes to Say* by Denise Brennan-Nelson

*Orange Pear Apple Bear* by Emily Gravett

*Tongue Twisters to Tangle Your Tongue* by Rebecca Cobb

*You Are My I Love You* by Maryann K. Cusimano

*You Are to Me* by Rebecca Doughty

**Activity #43: Poetry Play**

"Animal Crackers" by Christopher Morley

*B Is for Baby: An Alphabet of Verses* by Myra Cohn Livingston

*The Bed Book* by Sylvia Plath

*Block City* by Robert Louis Stevenson

"Hiding" by Dorothy Aldis

*I Never Did That Before* by Lilian Moore

*In Aunt Giraffe's Green Garden* by Jack Prelutsky

*Over in the Pink House: New Jump Rope Rhymes* by Rebecca Kai Dotlich

**Activity #45: Doctor Play**

*Alexander's Pretending Day* by Bunny Crumpacker

*Froggy Goes to the Doctor* by Jonathan London

*Next Please* by Ernest Jandl

**Activity #48: Mini-Museum**

*Behind the Museum Door: Poems to Celebrate the Wonder of Museums* by Lee Bennett Hopkins (ed.)

*Hannah's Collections* by Marthe Jocelyn

*How to Take Your Grandmother to the Museum* by Lois Wyse and Molly Rose Goldman

*Matthew's Dream* by Leo Lionni

**Activity #49: Spelling Fun**

*Hop on Pop* by Dr. Seuss